ZILLIONS

TITANIA'S BOOK OF NUMEROLOGY

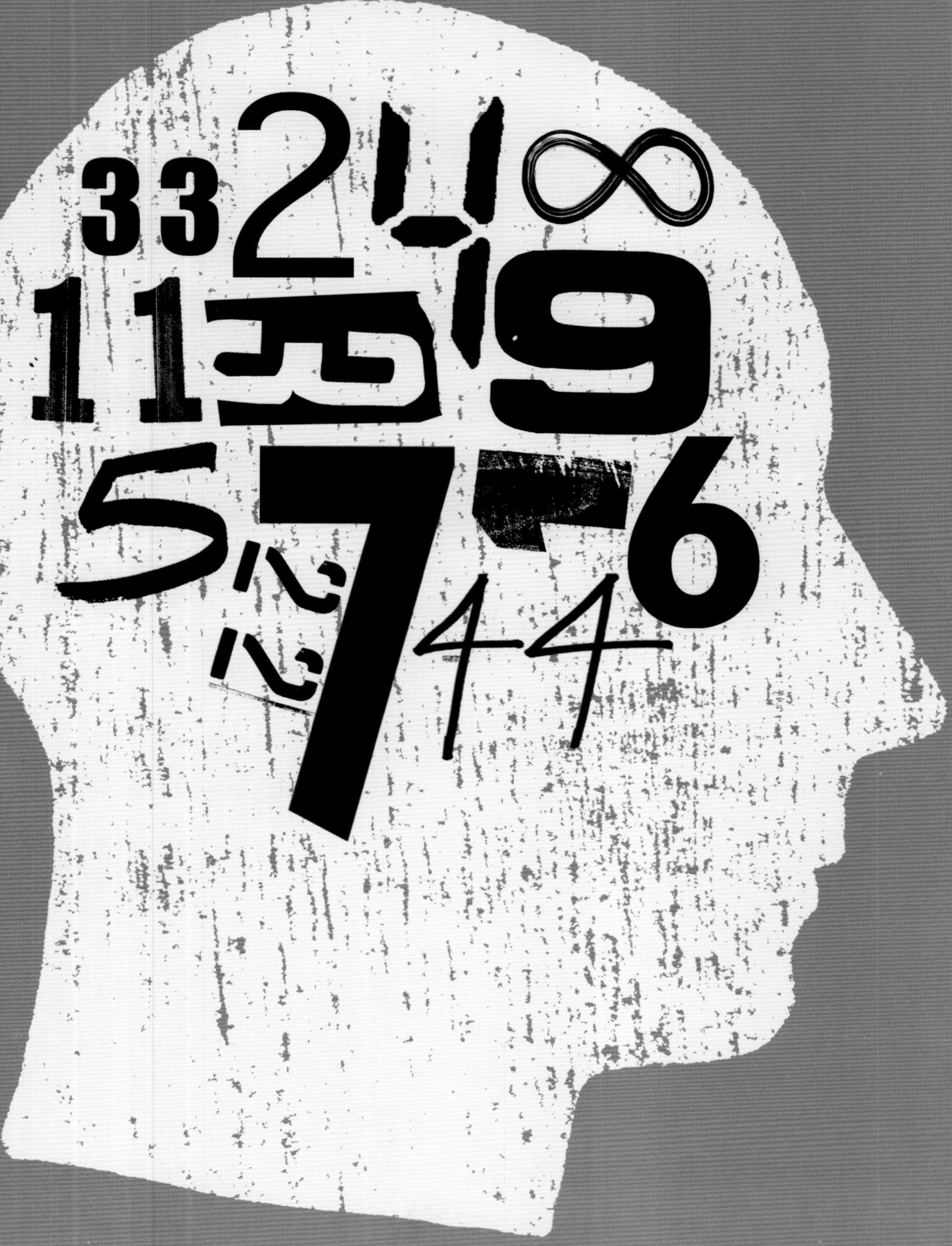

33
2
∞
11
9
5
7
6
44

ZILLIONS

TITANIA'S BOOK OF NUMEROLOGY

TITANIA HARDIE

ILLUSTRATIONS BY SHONAGH RAE

QUADRILLE PUBLISHING

This book is for some special mums and daughters who go back a long way: for Georgia Tilley, who taught me to count like this, and her girls, Sophia and Olivia; to Marcia Hines and Denni and Esmerelda in Sydney, who forgive my poor correspondence with warmth every time we do talk; to Brenda and Daria, who have helped out at crucial moments; to Mary Ellen and Kate who taught me to want to be a mum with a wonderful daughter too; and to my babies, the incomparable Samantha and Zephyrine, who repay all that is given 'up to the sky'. I also send this wish for wonder to all the lovely witchy ladies (of all generations) I have met in the last two or three years in bookshops and at events around the globe. 2000 is the moment we've been waiting for!

"WHEN ONE READS OF A WITCH BEING DUCKED, OF A WOMAN POSSESSED BY DEVILS, OF A WISE WOMAN SELLING HERBS, OR EVEN OF A VERY REMARKABLE MAN WITH A MOTHER, THEN I THINK WE ARE ON THE TRACK OF A LOST NOVELIST, A SUPPRESSED POET, OF SOME MUTE AND INGLORIOUS JANE AUSTEN."

Virginia Woolf, from her address To Cambridge Women, 1928.

Also by Titania Hardie

HOCUS POCUS Titania's Book of Spells

BEWITCHED Titania's Book of Love Spells

TITANIA'S ORAQLE A Unique way to Predict your Future

ENCHANTED Titania's Book of White Magic

TITANIA'S WISHING SPELLS Health

TITANIA'S WISHING SPELLS Wealth

TITANIA'S WISHING SPELLS Love

TITANIA'S WISHING SPELLS Happiness

TITANIA'S FORTUNE CARDS

All published by QUADRILLE

First published in 2000 by Quadrille Publishing Limited

Alhambra House, 27-31 Charing Cross Road, London WC2H 0LS

Reprinted 2000

10 9 8 7 6 5 4 3 2

PUBLISHING DIRECTOR Anne Furniss

DESIGN johnson banks

ASSISTANT EDITOR Emma Noble

PRODUCTION Sarah Tucker

© TEXT Titania Hardie 2000

© ILLUSTRATIONS Shonagh Rae 2000

© DESIGN AND LAYOUT Quadrille Publishing Limited 2000

BRITISH LIBRARY CATALOGUING IN PUBLICATION DATA

A catalogue record for this book is available from the British Library

ISBN 1 902757 60 2

PRINTED AND BOUND IN HONG KONG BY DAI NIPPON

Contents

Introduction   Page 6

Working out your numbers   Page 8

2

6

Page 10

Page 22

Page 34

Page 46

Page 58

Page 70

Page 82

Page 94

Page 106

Page 118

Page 130

Page 140

Compatibility between numbers   Page 142

Order your personalised
numerology chart from Titania   Page 144

INTRODUCTION

Did you know that if you're numerologically a number 7 you can't bear to lend anyone your toothbrush? And you like to leave your dinner plate spotlessly clean... If you're a 6 you can't cope with arguments in the home and do anything to avoid confrontations. If 1 is your number you must have some time alone each day or you'll go mad, while a 4 needs to keep busy doing something with their hands. A 9 gets on with just about anybody, and 8s can't help liking expensive things. 2s are musical; 3s stay young forever; 5s are great company, but can't sit still for ten minutes. 11s and 22s are brilliant Master Numbers – but quite bossy as well. So what number are you?

In an age that depends so wholly on computers, technology and numeracy, we can learn amazing lessons from the numbers that embody so much of our identity in symbolic ways. And with a change of millennium, a whole new implication arrives with the new date. The past thousand years has been prefixed in year date with the number 1, the male number, suggesting not only a period of male dominance, but actually of women being elided from thought and history. The welcome arrival of the number 2 in the new millennium embraces a more sharing, feminine ideal of co-operation and consideration of another party.

In our daily lives, who could doubt the importance of numbers? A quick glance will show the extraordinary 'coincidence' of how many family members, for instance, share a birthdate: not necessarily in the same month, but siblings may be born under the influence of the same number, so that one is born on the 2nd of a month, another on the 20th. I will show you that these numbers reduce to the same digit – 2 – and that many family members have numbers that overlap in this way. As you come to understand how to work out your numbers from these pages you will discover that many of your closest friends, and partners, have a number in common with you.

All the calculations we need to unravel our personalities, our lovers' inclinations, our chances of compatibility in a relationship, and indeed our future, can be derived primarily from our birthdate. The letters of the alphabet are also significant, but the most important sums are based on the numbers of our actual birthday, for this is the day on which we chose to enter an organic planet, an existing world.

In each chapter of this book we will look in depth at one number: its properties if it is a Day Force or a Birth Force, how it can help us to understand those we have relationships with, what it means as a number for our employer or employee, our houses or pets, and, as well, what kind of experience we will have in any given year in the future, under the influence of each individual number.

Numerology does not make us what we are; but it is a wonderful symbolic language which helps us to understand complex aspects of ourselves and others. It has been studied by many fine intellects throughout the ages and, in this new millennium, it can show us new possible dimensions of self-expression and analysis. The journey ahead should be both fascinating and illuminating.

WORKING OUT YOUR NUMBERS

For all the equations that unlock the secrets of numerology, you will need to write out your birthdate in full (or that of the person whose numbers you are calculating). Then you simply put a plus sign (+) between every digit, and add up all the numbers.

Birth Force: in the birthdate 2nd November 1968, you would write: $2+11+1+9+6+8 = 37$. Now further reduce this, adding, $3+7 = 10$, and again, $1+0 = 1$. So, the birthdate's total number, called the Birth or Life Force number, is 1.

Day Force: you also need the numbers of your birthday for another vital number: this is the Day Force. For this we need only add together the numbers of the day on which you were born, disregarding totally the month and the year. In the example above, the Day Force on 2nd is 2+ nothing: just 2. If the date had been 20th, you would add 2+0, and arrive again at 2.

So, the Day Force for the above birthday is 2, the Birth Force 1. You need both of these numbers, as you shall see, to understand fully your life and potentialities.

Master Numbers: if at any point in your calculations you are left with the numbers 11 or 22, you need no further reduction. These are Master Numbers, not reduced to 2 and 4. If your birthdate total (Birth Force) produces a 33 or 44, this, too, is relevant, and they are Master Numbers, but they don't have such a wide application, or as accepted a significance, as 11 and 22. This, then, is the centre of all your personal arithmetic.

THE SIGNIFICANCE OF THE DAY FORCE NUMBER

This number – that of the day of whichever month you were born – is, to my mind, the most important number of all. When we react to any situation instinctively, we do so with the personality traits of our Day Force, as this is, in a sense, our day-to-day number. It has a bearing on our natural talents, choice of colours and individual style, and the way other people see us in frequent situations. In many ways even the people closest to us only know us slightly, and it is this 'daily' side of us they see most often.

THE SIGNIFICANCE OF THE BIRTH FORCE

This number takes time to show its mark. We need to see its influence over many years, and to understand that it is, in a sense, representative of certain strengths and weaknesses that we have to learn to live with over the course of our life and experience. Many of these characteristics will only be revealed over time, so it can take years for us to come to know ourselves truly. Uncovering the aspects in our character of the Birth Force number is part of that process of discovery; so it can often be that we don't fully recognise the characteristics of this number as readily in ourselves as those of the Day Force. It remains to be seen over time how much we grow into, and fulfil, the potentials of this complex number.

YOUR LOVER

Each chapter deals in detail with the characteristics of the Day Force and Birth Force governed by this particular number. In addition, you will also find a heading, Your Lover, for each individual number. This is concerned with the characteristics of that individual number in love. When you are looking at the character of your lover, use both their Day Force and Birth

Force numbers to understand their full character. Your beloved will behave for the most part as a true-to-form Day Force number; but, over the years, you will see the deeper side of his or her character based also on their Birth Force number. Thus both numbers are important.

YOUR CHILD

When you are looking at the section on Your Child, consult both their Day Force and Birth Force numbers: so, if your child is a Day Force 3 and a Birth Force 6, look up both the 3 child and the 6 child, being aware that the Day Force number will assert itself predominantly, but that over the course of their lifetime, the Birth Force will be revealed more completely.

FUTURE YEAR CYCLES

Each year, on our birthday, a new number cycle is initiated. We never stop being affected most by our Day and Birth Force numbers, but each new birthday cycle kicks off a year spent under the temporary but highly significant influence of this extra number. In the years when this coincides with our Birth Force number, it will be a really important year.

Every year you can determine what number will rule your energies by taking the numbers of your own birth day and month (but not year) and adding them to those of the year we are currently in. So, if you were born on 2nd November, you add 2+11, then omit your year of birth and add instead the numbers of the current year (let's use 2000). Thus, add 2+11+2+0+0+0 = 15. Then reduce to one digit as usual, to arrive at 1+5 = 6. These calculations reveal that you would be under a 6 year cycle from 2nd November 2000 until the eve of your birthday in 2001. Note that the number cycle doesn't actually begin until your birthday. A January birthday will produce a year cycle starting very close to the calendar year of 2000; a December birthday won't show real effect until December, when the year 2000 is ironically almost over, but its influence will continue until the following December.

COMPATIBILITY

The only other important calculation you need worry about is your compatibility with other numbers. There is a detailed explanation of this on pages 142-3, showing in brief the compatibility of every number with all the other numbers. When calculating your compatibility, which is on a day-to-day basis with almost everyone we meet, the Day Force number is the principal number to influence us. If you are in a long-term relationship you might like to compare Birth Force numbers as well.

THE ALPHABET

All the letters of the alphabet have a numerical value, which can be seen in the chart below. At the beginning and end of each chapter the letters attributed to that number are mentioned and a little is said about them.

1	2	3	4	5	6	7	8	9
a	b	c	d	e	f	g	h	i
j	k*	l	m	n	o	p	q	r
s	t	u	v**	w	x	y	z	

* 'k', given a value of 2, is the only letter corresponding to Master Number 11;
**'v', usually given as 4, really corresponds to Master Number 22.

10

ONE

NUMBER OF COURAGE, INDIVIDUALITY, AND AGGRESSION, 1 IS THE BEGINNING OF OUR JOURNEY. IT REPRESENTS THE INITIATIVE TO START EVERYTHING — IT IS DYNAMIC ENERGY, THOUGHT, AND WILL. TO BE A 1 IN ANY FORM TELLS OTHERS YOU ARE HUGELY INDEPENDENT AND SELF-RELIANT. YET, TOO, IT IS A NUMBER OF SUFFERING — FOR NOT EVERYONE WHO IS INDEPENDENT ALSO WISHES TO BE ALL ALONE.

IF THIS IS ONE OF YOUR NUMBERS, OR IF YOU SHARE A HOUSE WITH A 1 PARTNER OR CHILD, THINGS WILL NEVER BE DULL. THIS NUMBER HATES INACTION AND LOVES TO STIR THINGS UP WHEN EVERYONE ELSE IS TIRED OUT OR PENSIVE. BOTH DETERMINED AND CONTRARY, CYNICAL AND INVENTIVE, 1S ARE FASCINATING AND CHARISMATIC, BUT HATE TO BE TOLD WHAT TO DO BY ANYONE ELSE — SO IT CAN BE A HIGH-WIRE ACT TIP-TOEING AROUND A 1'S DELICATE EGO.

AS A 1 YOUR COLOURS ARE FLAME, COPPER, AND APRICOT; YOUR SCENTS ARE ROSE OTTO, CEDARWOOD, CYPRESS, AND CORIANDER (FOR CONFIDENCE AND SELF-ASSERTION); YOUR ASTROLOGICAL EQUIVALENT IS ARIES; AND THE LETTERS A, J AND S RESONATE TO THE NUMBER 1, SO YOU NEED TO USE A NAME WITH ONE OF THESE LETTERS PROMINENT IF YOU ARE TO ENJOY THE TRUE BENEFITS OF STRENGTH AND SELF-RELIANCE THAT GO WITH THIS STRONG NUMBER.

DAY FORCE 1

In the introduction it was explained that your Day Force number is taken from just the day on which you were born, disregarding the month and year. Thus, 1 is your Day Force if your birthdate is the 1st, 10th, 19th or 28th of any month. The Day Force exerts its influence each and every day of your life. It is this number which determines our individual and immediate reaction to everyday situations and how we will respond to issues that arise with our lovers and friends, family, business associates and authority figures. Thus, with any of the above birthdays, you react as a 1.

ALL 1 BIRTHDAYS

Whichever 1 is your actual birthdate, you are a force to be reckoned with – a whirlwind of thought and activity. You have wonderful powers of concentration and inventiveness, and a sense of daring that amazes even those who know you best throughout your life. You need no-one's example to follow, are happy to plunge in when circumstances are not yet revealed, and have the courage to walk into 'dark' situations – making a light, indeed, for others to follow.

Your memory is excellent and you recall even the most complex conversations in detail. You 'never say die'. This frequently compels you not only to lead, but to invent activities and undertakings for others. You require business positions of executive status or self-employment and you will prefer work that allows you to think out, explore, develop and plan, rather than physical labour or mundane, routine work.

You don't mean to be boastful, but you can't help reminding others that you find no difficulty where they find obstacles all the time. You literally create your own opportunities, so you have little time for people who get stuck for inspiration or lack motivation and the will to climb out of personal doldrums. Sometimes you become bossy and bully friends who have lost their way. However, if they know you well they come, not for tea and sympathy, but for a well-timed kick in the butt to get them going again!

You concentrate wonderfully and work to the point of exhaustion until you can see things established. Thereafter, others must come in and nurse it for you: once an idea has proved itself do-able, you lose interest and must leave the routine work to associates. Your excitement is in proving the possibility, so you must choose a very steady business partner or assistant. In matters of the heart, your beloved will need to understand this impatience in you.

Many events in life will force you to use your excellent strengths and talents – sometimes quite suddenly and strangely. Even in childhood you will have been urged to stand on your own two feet and show adult inclinations: 1s often seem to be deprived of a truly gentle childhood. But this is requisite to your daily need to show independence and authority – you have been learning how to do this almost from the cradle.

In relationships of love, you are in need of a very understanding and perhaps highly intuitive partner. You sometimes need to be alone, to think, to create, to unwind from your own extraordinary energy. But you are sensitive to criticism from others and badly need their approval. Aggression is often a camouflage for a feeling of being alone or having to carry too much of the burden for others. Everyone seems to lean on you and perhaps not realise that you need someone to listen to you too.

Choose a partner (ideally) who is patient, quite independent themselves, and good at reading between the lines. They will have to learn to cuddle you without actually being asked to do so: be aware that this is sometimes quite difficult.

Birthday on 1st

With this birthday, you are dynamic, original, impulsive and strong-willed; the most inspired starter who lacks the patience to finish the job, preferring to leave the back-up tasks to others.

You are somewhat reticent and undemonstrative emotionally, but need praise and encouragement yourself. You are an intellectual, and need several lines of pursuit simultaneously to hold your interest. You are very independent and motivated, but you also need a lot of time alone. You feel misunderstood by those who think you can stand by yourself without support. Of course you are a great survivor, but ask for assistance, at least sometimes.

Watch a tendency to dominate others, and guard against jealousy in relationships of both love and friendship. Also, do try to listen to advice: you can always reject others' ideas, but it is illuminating to listen. Separate your emotions from your intellect and make objective decisions. You are practical and powerful, idealistic and imaginative.

Your emotions, once engaged, run very deep. You love companionship and celebrate wildly when in the mood; but some people think you unaffectionate, so you can spend too much time on your own. Communicate your real needs to friends and lovers who can't always read your deep and complex personality.

You have many career options: a gift for inspirational teaching; for acting – enjoying the moment alone in the spotlight; for any form of inventing; for design. You definitely need to work independently.

Birthday on 10th

Zero increases some of the 1 tendencies tenfold. You are independent and self-reliant, sometimes bossy, and naturally assume the lead. Your energies are aggressive in the best sense; yours is a voice to be heard. You will never be walked over.

You are able and willing to stand alone; throughout your life people will lean on you and seek you out for your strength and boldness. Others seek your advice, but they know less well how to help you. They see you as self-sufficient and admire your strength of character. And indeed, you have original ideas about life and business, taking your cue from no-one, discovering your mistakes through hard-earned knocks. You do prefer, in all honesty, to go it alone most of the time, and rather than ask for what you want from others, do the job yourself. You are not good at taking orders from others. Though surprisingly gentle, you are nevertheless stubborn about the way to approach a problem and like to follow your own advice.

You probably work for yourself and not in a nine-to-five capacity. You are idealistic, full of clever ideas about how to improve the world around you. You initiate changes at work and home, finding fresh approaches to stale situations and pushing everyone to greater exertion. You could manage several businesses at one time, or follow several lines of endeavour at once. This way, you bring at least one of your pet projects to fruition even if the others go nowhere.

You are likely to be gifted in music, possibly in painting or architecture. You re-invent everyday items to make them better. You are clever, original, strong-minded, jealous of possessions and friends. Most females with this birthdate are not only strong but lack all inclination for the role of female domesticity.

BIRTHDAY ON 19TH

This number has wonderful artistic talent, a nice sense of humour and a capacity to set trends. However, it is also a 'karmic debt number': you have some lesson to learn harking back to another life and you will be forced to stand alone again and again from childhood to your final years. This often suggests emotional extremes and you may find yourself vacillating between buoyant optimism and moody pessimism. You will have to work hard not to indulge yourself by wallowing in despair for too long.

You love change, relish private time and resent too much intrusion from company; though when you are in the mood for friends, no-one is a better or funnier host. People may think your ideas mad sometimes, but usually you have the last laugh.

Like all 1s you can be nervous and irritable, or quick to anger, but you are just as quick to recover your temper and forgive. You set yourself high standards to live by – and expect others to follow suit. You may be in danger of missing out on complete happiness in relationships because of a tendency to withdraw into your own world and appear thoroughly self-sufficient. You can be misunderstood because of this and you must find a way of asking for what you need or desire.

Versatility dictates that you will succeed in different fields, or try more than one profession. Part of you wants to be in the limelight and part wants to work privately, unwatched, at your own areas of interest. This latter streak will predominate if your Birth Force is 7.

Career choices include politics and law, perhaps medicine, or physically demanding jobs like dance, aerobics instruction, sport, design, or teaching at a high level. You love to work odd hours and for yourself, and need something new to get your teeth into from time to time.

BIRTHDAY ON 28TH

This date makes you a true individual. This version of 1 symbolises high ideals and standards, huge self will and, rather differently from the other 1s, a capacity for really deep affection. You are still very independent and quite dominant and need no-one to sanction your actions and beliefs; but you are able to sacrifice some of your drive to self-sufficiency on the path to emotional contentment (thanks to the 2 in your birthdate of 28) and fit ambition and relationship together better than many of the 1s.

Your relationships and friendships are sometimes unconventional. You love truly, and are a charismatic partner. You start lots of projects but often lose interest once things are up and running; preferring instead to delegate.

You must have freedom and chafe at limitations. You are incredibly single-minded and can wait quite patiently until the time is ripe to propel yourself into action. You may be guilty of magnifying your problems beyond reality and you should guard against exaggeration to the point of self-delusion. Watch out for regular lapses into laziness or conceit and don't waste too much time dreaming up plans: your destiny should be to achieve.

You are the leader, the executive, the affable up-front spokesperson. You are prepared to stand alone if need be and ready to assert your rights as well as those of others. Among a group of independent thinkers you will be the leader. You will teach well and may choose this as a career, but you will expect the best from your students. You could also choose a path in law, or self-employment, or again, any vocation which demands physical energy. This has been the birthday of many kings.

BIRTH FORCE 1

The daily (or Day Force) number influences all your immediate and obvious actions on a day-to-day basis, whereas your Birth Force number (sometimes called the Life Lesson number) is a number you grow into during your lifetime. Therefore, unlike the day number which begins to assert itself from childhood, it may take some time to see the true vein of this number manifesting itself in your character. To find your Birth Force number, add together all the numbers of your day, month and year of birth and reduce them to a single digit.

A Birth Force number of 1 indicates that your path in life is to learn to be independent, to find a role of leadership and authority, to grow into a preference for privacy, to stand alone when required. You must be prepared to forge ahead relentlessly and not to lose courage or turn back. This can sometimes be a lonely road and you will be asked time and again to be responsible for yourself. You somehow project an image of confidence and calm; in truth, you do have a well-developed sense of what will turn out well.

You have excellent physical skills and agility, as well as a good sense of timing, and these strengths may be called upon in your journey to reach your own individual destiny – sometimes in odd ways. You will always find new audiences prepared to listen to your original ideas, and will find many different outlets for your self-expression. This means changes of vocation, or a leisure interest which eventually becomes more than a pastime.

You are looked to by others to take the lead and may be seen by some people as a pioneer or even a bit of an oddball, but you will be followed in a crisis. You will find over time that you work best alone, though it will be a challenge to learn to co-operate with the people around you. You must recognise that you are not always automatically right: try to listen to others.

Birth Force 1 is a male number, so sometimes women carrying this number are seen as masculine and aggressive. It is also an active number, and you may become a determined and courageous person. You may be thrust into positions of authority, but you are equipped for this and will eventually relish the role.

You may be compared by friends and loved ones more with your father than your mother because of the masculine principle of this number. Many female 1s find themselves caught between the rival urges of nurturing a family and competing in a business world. Somehow they find a way, but it can take years to feel they are not failing at one role or the other.

If this is your total number, you must learn to be selective in your relationships: you need to find a partner who understands your impatience to achieve in life, who can play second fiddle to you when required. This will best be achieved if your partner is also self-motivated and quietly confident: you may not mean to neglect those you love, but sometimes, you do. You are, however, bound to be one of life's achievers, looked up to by those who know you. Ask for help from your loved ones when you need it, instead of expecting them to guess. It might also help to be aware that, much as they love you, they do sometimes see you as a bit of a know-it-all and can lose patience with you as a result.

Much of your personal sense of style is dictated by your Birth Force number: this is how the world seems to see you. You project outward capability and self-sufficiency; you present a positive image and you are highly individual in your fashion sense and taste. You probably prefer designer clothes, or unusual items, and hate to dress like everyone else. Your choice of colour may be daring and you are unafraid to draw attention to yourself by your choice of attire. You may even choose clothes and interior decoration just to shock.

YOUR 1 LOVER

Partners born under this strongly independent number will stretch your sense of self-confidence and demand that you acquire great intuitive skills to read them well. 1s never really admit how desperately they need approval – and affection – from those closest to them, giving instead the sometimes unwitting impression that they are totally self-sufficient and jealous of their privacy. This means you need to see beyond this, understanding in fact that there is a very small child inside every number 1, male or female, and that this child needs lots of cuddles and gentle signs of your encouragement in all things.

On the bright side, you've been attracted to a highly original soul, wonderfully charismatic, someone who truly stands out in a crowd. If you're honest, that enigmatic, self-determined personality is part of what intrigues you. This capable, creative person will never be dull; you may also have an unusual courtship, doing things you've never tried before. You'll enjoy private time together, company never being requisite to your combined happiness. On the other hand, your 1 has such a magnetic personality that friends will gravitate to you both.

Your 1 has many intelligent and different perspectives to offer you on life and loves to be amongst the first to try out new things. His or her wardrobe will be individual and full of one-offs (budget permitting): 1s never dress the same way as others. They will take control of most situations (even when you didn't want them to) and image is crucial. Be sensitive to this when you are about to criticise, and choose your words extremely carefully.

Have you got the impression of someone with a fragile (but strong) ego? This is certainly true; and your 1 love is also wilful and impulsive. Seen positively, this means that indecision is rarely a problem, for 1s know what they want and grab it immediately, relegating commonsense issues of affordability to the rear. On the negative side, you may find it grating when you feel your partner knows it all and never really acknowledges the part you play. Or worse, you're not quite sure you're even needed: your 1 is so private and emotionally guarded, so dislikes restraint of any kind, that you feel insecure and uncertain of where the relationship is going.

Remember that loving this natural leader, this true character who has so much assertiveness, is not for the faint-hearted. Develop tactful means of phrasing your requests, don't give in to frustrated tempers and try to diffuse tense situations with humour – for meeting a 1 in head-on confrontation will be explosive and probably not very productive. If your 1 is simply too selfish and uncaring, don't be hopeful that this is going to change. But if you can manage the sometimes lonely path, or wondering what to expect next, you'll be rewarded with a lover who has extraordinary, original observations to share with you, an exciting intellect, a brilliant imagination and a pioneer's enthusiasm for new possibilities. You'll be much envied by most of your friends, and something unexpected will happen at every turn.

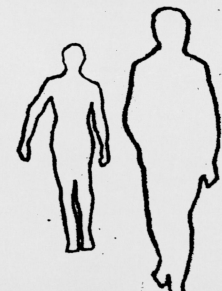

THE 1 CHILD

Your 1 child needs sensitive handling. Here is a young mind full of energy and interest, with too many questions and an instinctive disinclination to authority. You have the difficult task of directing your child's natural feeling of independence and self-worth while discouraging the potential selfishness and arrogance that often come with the number. Placing parameters is also hard: a 1 child really chafes against restraint of any kind, sometimes to their own detriment. They have to learn to live in a social world and recognise that they are not always right.

Help them to build their unique personality by treating them, as far as possible, as an adult. Give them your time and listen to their interesting ideas and observations about people and situations. They have a wish to be dominant among friends and within the family and it is vital that you gently steer them toward positive expressions for their goals and also towards tolerance of the needs of others.

The hardest thing to read, again, is their cry for company, which is often hidden by an appearance of brash self-confidence and a wish for privacy. Your 1 child does require time alone, to think, to create, to invent; but he or she also needs someone to guess when they just want a hug. Be aware that inherent stubbornness and a belief in going it alone makes it difficult for them to ask outright for these signs of affection.

THE 1 BOSS

Let's hope you're a patient soul. Your 1 employer is dynamic and exciting, but only one opinion is right – and it's always his or hers. On the credit side you will learn a great deal about chutzpah, daring and that no such word as impossibility exists in the dictionary; on the debit side, you will be relied upon to pick up all the follow-on tasks, but often not thanked for your good-humoured diligence.

THE 1 EMPLOYEE

Here is someone with their eye on the top job, whatever they say. This character is not prepared to tow the line for long, so if they work for you the best you can hope for is their self-reliance and initiative; the worst scenario is that they'll completely ignore whatever you say about the way to tackle things – you're playing with fire.

THE 1 LETTERS

If the name you use contains rather a lot of 1 letters – As, Js and/or Ss – and especially if your first initial is one of these, you contain many qualities of number 1 by proxy. You have a good intellect, enjoy your own company, produce many original ideas and are also a little self-opinionated and headstrong. A has great self-reliance and initiative; J, profound honesty and inventive ability; and S, both charm and anger, as well as a love of money.

THE 1 HOUSE

If you live in a house whose number reduces to 1, you will find you have a very individual abode. It will be decorated entirely differently from otherwise seemingly identical neighbours, but it has attracted you to live there because of its individuality. The interesting thing is that those who dwell in 1 houses often spend a lot of time there on their own.

THE 1 PET

If your pet is a 1, be prepared to be amazed. This animal – be it dog, cat, horse, rabbit or python – will forever choose the opposite of what you offer, sleep in bizarre places, show incredible independence and determination and perhaps allow you to become its close friend. This pet also displays a dazzling sense of humour.

WHAT HAPPENS IN A 1 YEAR?

Every year we can calculate the year cycle we are entering if we add up our whole birthdate, but replace our birth year (such as 1970) with the year we are in now (such as 2001). In effect, it is like a replacement Birth Force number, but operative only for each twelve-month period. The number comes into play from the birthday itself, rather than the New Year: so, if you have an April birthday, your new year cycle begins each new April.

If you add up the digits of your birthday this year and arrive at a total of 1, you are about to start a whole new nine-year cycle of your life. This is the moment to set new, specific long-term goals, and to consider carefully where you want to be a few years from now. You are bound to have new people around you from this point on and new ideas in relation to this. In a sense, this begins a new chapter in your life.

In business terms, a 1 year will often occur at a time of new employment, or of a complete change in direction from one vocational path to another. This is a time during which it is not so difficult to step back and see how to embark on a course of action, or see a goal as perfectly attainable, when only a year or so ago it seemed pure fantasy. In a 1 year you have tremendous focus, independence, and excellent determination: now, you are thinking for yourself.

You may have to stand alone in some way and your relationships (especially one) will alter during this twelve-month period. It is absolutely possible that one relationship recently ended (during the previous nine-year cycle) and that you are enjoying a temporary moment of freedom in this go-it-alone year. It is equally possible that, having played the field a little until now, you suddenly find one special love rises to prominence during the influence of this 1 year. Emotionally, a 1 year is always a fresh start, even if this is within the relationship you have had for a long time.

While this cycle lasts you will have lots of original, interesting ideas, as well as the will to act on them. You seem to be more self-assured now and won't allow others to talk you down. Whatever ambition you've lighted upon, you can genuinely attain; you have an enviable single-mindedness and great powers of restraint and control. You don't find decisions so hard to reach,-and you are quite prepared to do things all by yourself if necessary. The one thing you must watch, though, is a tendency during this cycle to be more blunt or tactless than usual and to be impulsive and unwilling to listen to any advice. You must find the balance between asserting your independence and individuality without being arrogant or irrational. On the other hand, your intuition is working very well and luck seems to favour the brave. There will almost certainly be a change of direction for you and any new path seems to herald a change for the best.

Be courageous. If you do find yourself spending some of this cycle on your own, this, too, will start to alter by the closing stages of the cycle, as you head into a 2 (or 11) year cycle next year. Looking back then, you will see that this was the foundation of all.

Two

This is the number of the peace-maker. 2 takes co-operation and team-work as an essential in life, along with the instinctive tendency to think of others.

2 is a feminine number, not in the sense that women should take second place, but that they are aware of others in the world and always consider themselves in relation to friends and loved ones. Traditionally it was a passive (though not inactive) number; the leading digit of the new millennium takes on the principles of this number with a consideration and feminine tact.

If 2 is one of your numbers you are probably self-conscious yet surprisingly stubborn. You need to work in agreement with those nearest you, and you look for details and gather all the facts. If you share a house with a 2 you know they are sensitive and easily hurt, sometimes shy, but very loyal. A 2 close to you will always consider your needs and opinions, but it will take time to arrive at simple decisions while they weigh everything up.

If you're a 2 you need to use a name with the letters B, K or T prominently, otherwise you may feel nervous and emotionally tense. Your colours are gold, salmon and prune; your scents are rose geranium, carnation and chamomile (for peace); and your astrological relative is Taurus.

23

Day Force 2

I have explained that your Day Force number is taken from those of the day of whichever month you are born, disregarding the year. So, in this case, 2 is your Day Force if your birthdate is the 2nd or 20th of any month. However, the key point to remember is that if your birthday is on the 11th or 29th of a month you are in fact not a 2, but a Master Number 11 instead. This number (along with 22) never reduces; so you should consult the chapter on number 11 if your birthday is on either of these days.

All 2 Birthdays

Remember that the Day Force exerts its influence each day of your life; this is the number which determines our individual and immediate reaction to everyday situations and how we will respond to issues that arise within all our relationships and business situations. So, if you were born on the 2nd or the 20th, you react as a 2.

You are a sensitive being, easily offended and emotionally touched, but also considerate and kind towards other people. Though sometimes shy with strangers, you are great company amongst your own friends. Your greatest strength is that you can touch people with your words and gently persuade them to your viewpoint – which is why you are so brilliant at making peace between disputatious souls.

You have an obvious sincerity in dealing with the world and a strongly spiritual side to your nature, so others trust you instinctively. You are also admired for your grace and aesthetic sense: you are musical and probably dance well, especially as one of a pair. You are the ideal team-mate and will probably find you work best in tandem, both creatively and in business, bouncing your ideas off someone you relate to well.

You will also appreciate all the beautiful and artistic things of life and, if inspired, probably be an absolute romantic. You are a deep feeler, and highly sensitive to your surroundings. This also means that one of your worst problems will be a tendency to mood swings and sudden depressions, which you must overcome if possible. This might partly be because you want and need affection, also because you sometimes underestimate your abilities and feel you must be 'needed' in a relationship rather than simply loved. This trait can lead you into situations which allow you to become a doormat for other people, but this will never give you a true sense of self-esteem.

You gain your needs in life by peaceful means, and understand that creating accord around you behoves you better than fighting. This outstanding gift of diplomacy and the capacity to mediate makes you a gentle force to be reckoned with, showing up the childish aggressions of those who prefer a more bullying approach. You control the situation through gentleness.

It is not uncommon for you to be quite exacting about standards of cleanliness and personal neatness, occasionally to the point of obsession. Your personal appearance is important to you, and you may make a fuss if things are not just right. Clothing is thus a preoccupation; and you may also make a mountain out of a mole hill with some imperfection of nose, hair or figure. At this level, you can be as self-critical as a 7.

Popularity, nevertheless, attends you: your kind, courteous charm ensures a line of lovers and many best friends, as well as the love of the family who know you. There is a magical property in the number 2; you will discover your powers in time.

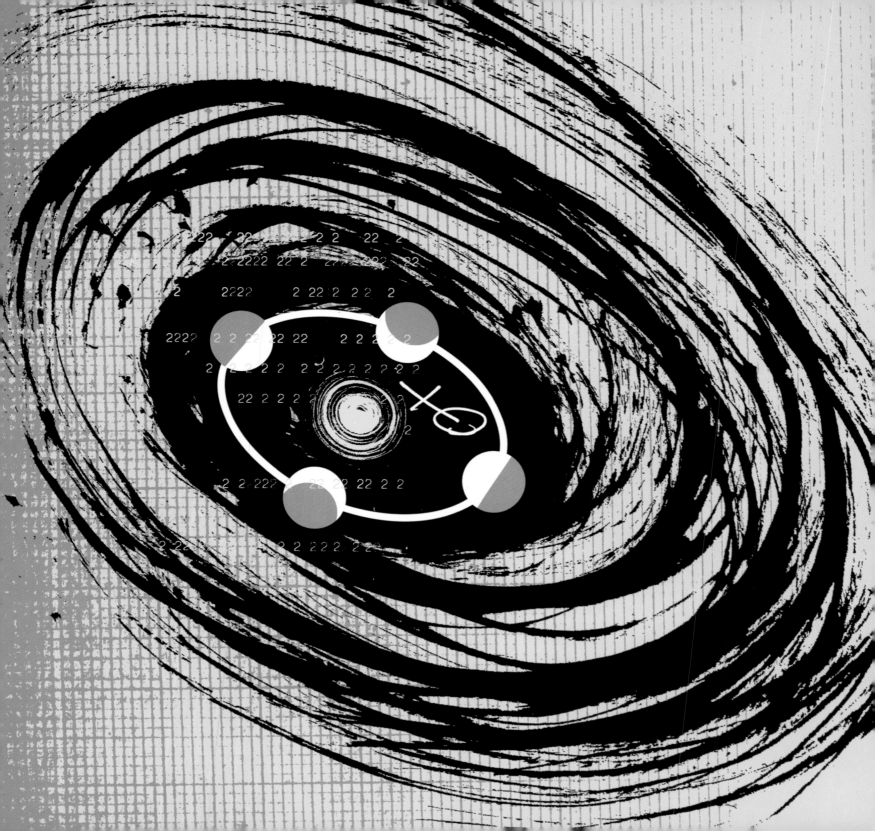

Birthday on 2nd

You are a pure 2 and have a natural wish to live peacefully, whether it be in love, with family and where you work. You achieve what you want through skilful diplomacy, without force or aggression of any kind, and your perspicacity ensures that you understand how to sway people gently and without commotion. You are not the outstanding executive type but the brilliant ambassador, accomplishing often what no-one else can in terms of mediation.

Everyone depends upon you to tell the truth, tactfully. You support friends in crisis without expecting overt gratitude and you add strength to love partnerships and with your children. You know how to soothe and encourage, but you are also usually very impartial, which makes you a good counsellor and friend to both sides. You like to be led, but you are not in the least weak. Rather, you have an astounding understanding of how to gain what you want without being too direct. So, aggressive souls who think you are a pushover are in for a shock.

You are a highly musical person, have an excellent ear and usually a gentle speaking voice. You also love beauty and create a visual oasis of calm around you, whether at work or at home. You work very well in partnership and have a knack for consulting those closest to you and incorporating their ideas and wishes into your own harmonious overview. You are easily able to discover ways of sharing space and taste to everyone's satisfaction.

The positions open to you in career terms are many. Because of your superb diplomatic and peacemaking nature, you 2s are excellent politicians and civil servants. Antiques, objects of beauty and areas of fashion or art are subjects that will appeal to you in business; and since you are the perfect co-worker you would be successful in any partnership, provided you choose the right field.

From an artistic point of view, poetry, writing, music, painting and sculpture will be your best suits. You should also be very good at taking on mundane tasks when required and bringing a degree of perfection and excellence to them: hence, bookkeeping, statistics, secretarial work or analytical subjects are all fields open to you. Whatever you choose, you will bring smiles to the faces of those who work around you.

Birthday on 20th

You are especially tactful and diplomatic, as well as strongly devoted to family and loved ones. The most gifted peacemaker, if you are at one with your positive energies you have the power to succeed at anything you're inclined to try, but if your upbringing and conditioning have made you negative, you will possibly be changeable and unreliable.

You have a particularly fine appreciation of music and of the arts, plus a beautiful, subtle feeling for colour. Your strongly loving nature could allow others to take advantage of you. You would be well suited for government work with your innate sense of diplomacy; but you are quite content to work in small groups or for others, tending not to push for your own business or personal supremacy. This sometimes means others take advantage of you, allowing you to do the difficult legwork, then pushing themselves forward to take all the credit.

You are loving and sympathetic; you enjoy nature, the countryside and your home. Just as you are good at bringing peace, you need to find peaceful places in order to recharge your battery and help you unwind from the stresses of modern living. Your personality, environment and way of doing things represents grace, style and beauty. An inharmonious dwelling place or office climate will make you very stressed and unhappy, preventing you from performing at your best.

Careerwise, you would succeed in any field of public work, in particular as an analyst, teacher (possibly of artistic or musical subjects) or actor; or, quite differently, as a clergyman, politician or statistician; or, again, as a musician, a clerk, or even a typist or stenographer. You would ideally make the best of politicians, but you may write more effectively than you speak. You can be extremely patient in handling detail, thus you could ably handle estates, or succeed in corporate law or politics.

The basic 2 element is with you tenfold: femininity (even in men, who are gentle beings with many women as friends), intuition and a giving nature; you will often place others before yourself. This birthday corresponds to the receptive female, moon principle. You co-operate with others by nature and are born to be in a loving pair, making you a real catch as a marriage partner.

BIRTH FORCE 2

Remember that, as distinct from the daily number (Day Force) which colours your immediate moods and actions on a day-to-day basis, your Birth Force number (alternatively called the Life Lesson number) is a number you grow into. Unlike the day number which asserts itself from your early life, it may take time to see the true characteristics of this number influencing your character and direction. To find your Birth Force number, add up all the numbers of your day, month and year of birth and reduce to a single digit.

Your Birth Force number 2 signifies that co-operation will be one of the main themes of your life, and that you will gradually become more and more sensitive to the needs, spoken or unspoken, of others in your life. You are often the unsung heroes of life, the power behind the throne of the more obviously successful 1s, 5s and 8s. You have learnt the art of tact, diplomacy and peacemaking and to become a good social mixer, as well as how to influence others in the quietest way.

You are rarely selfish, yet you develop a stubborn streak with time and eventually learn not to be pushed about by others. You would do well in a business partnership, especially as you do not seek self-praise. Your sincerity and graciousness are marvellous assets in business and you gently acquire the things in life you yearn for without brutality or overt aggression. The associates you help on the road to their achievements will usually acknowledge the contributive role you have played.

You cultivate friendships easily, knowing when to be kind, generous and loyal. You steadily learn to work diligently without thought of reward; fate appears to see to your needs. You are gifted at bringing diverse people together for a common cause, naturally sniffing out details and undertaking research to be of service to others. You have probably learned how to hold your tongue, realising that speech is silver but silence is gold. When necessary, however, you are a gentle and persuasive talker, who may be asked to act as a go-between for hostile factions.

Your skills, unfolding through your life, are artistic. Career paths will extend to music, research, business partnerships of all kinds, auditing and acting as an agent for others. Even if you take your career direction from your Day Force number, your strengths in these areas will grow and, at the very least, provide a leisure interest. Your capacity for diplomacy will be evident in any job you take, and you are certain to work in partnership with others, or with another whom you admire.

Of course you have faults, too, which will emerge over time. You can easily give in to negativity, fear and even timidity. Worst of all, perhaps, you hate making mistakes, and this sometimes inhibits you from taking any action at all, for fear you will achieve less than perfect results. You must also control your tendency to extremes, particularly emotionally. You have strong likes and dislikes, but you should fight the mood swings which make others unsure of you.

You are likely to be neat and clean, concerned with health and hygiene (especially if 7 is your other number), and you are organised in your work. You probably prefer a dress style, too, which is neat, well-fitted, with subtle, balancing colours. Easy, comfortable styles are perfect for you, yet you manage to make quiet garments effortlessly graceful.

In a love relationship, find someone who appreciates your kindness and won't let you become too self-sacrificing. Make sure, too, that your lover is a good dancer, or likes music: this is an important part of your life and, of course, you love to do things in tandem.

YOUR 2 LOVER

Lucky you! This divine soul is gentle, caring and co-operative, happy to consult you on your own needs and wants; sensitive enough to know when you want to be left alone and when you need to talk. You will rely on your 2's intuition in all matters and be glad of their warm, supportive manner, which is as attractive to your family and friends as it is to you.

Your 2 is musical and you'll need a good pair of dancing shoes to keep up with him or her. Your lives together will definitely incorporate music and aesthetic pleasures; you will make a harmonious home, which your 2 will help to run smoothly and neatly. Give them a free rein with decorative ideas, for they have a sensitive eye for colour and know how to bring different elements together to make them work as a unit.

A 2 lover is a sensuous partner, who needs time to relax you on the sofa or in the bedroom: don't hurry him or her. Here is someone with gentle, caring hands who enjoys making contact with you and finding out how you feel. You will share a bedroom with peaceful, harmonizing colours, clean sheets, and gentle music. A female 2 will provide sweet-smelling treats and oils; a male 2 is likely to bring a drop of something nice to drink into your love-making space... mmm... delicious.

Your 2 partner will pick you up for a date in sensible shoes and smart, freshly cleaned clothes – but dazzling diamante, never. This is not someone concerned with making a big entrance, but it is someone who will have taken care of more important details such as great food, a seductive ambience at a restaurant, probably somewhere to dance – so you see, those sensible shoes were well-advised. For holidays, choose a peaceful retreat together, preferably a watery paradise. Mood is all and, though you have a co-operative character here, you will please him or her effortlessly if you find a place to go which favours romance over action.

Are there no blemishes on this paragon? Of course, you will have to beware the unexpected mood swing, the words you speak that for some reason deeply offend this sensitive nature and the days after a quarrel when your 2 goes to ground to think out what to do. Or, if he or she has had a terrible day at work, watch those irritatingly over-conscientious habits around the house, along with a determination to be unhappy. But, best for last, a 2 is the ideal marriage partner: good at working things out, this is a teamworker who knows there are two sides to everything... definitely one to keep for life.

THE 2 CHILD

Here is a very sensitive little one. From infancy you will realise he or she has a way of very quietly getting just what they want, their sweetness being no cover for their persuasive streak. This is also quite a telepathic little person from whom it is impossible to keep anything. Listen, too, to his or her intuition about friends and business associates, for their instincts are uncannily accurate.

Your 2 child will hate warfare in the home, so try not to have disputes within their sensitive environment: if there is a family quarrel, the 2 will do everything to heal the breach and bring everyone into accord. Your natural peacemaker will carry this skill into their adult life and could turn this attribute to good advantage – in a government post as civil servant or diplomat, or to riches in a business partnership.

A 2 child should be encouraged to develop fully a natural talent for music, painting and dance, regardless of gender. Allow your 2 a peaceful place of their own to go and sit thoughtfully and unwind. Be sure never to take their emotional troubles lightly: they become deeply attached to friends and first loves, so you need to take this seriously, and counsel patiently and wisely.

THE 2 BOSS

An easy, co-operative soul, this is someone who should be a pleasure to work with. You'll always be acknowledged for the contributions you make to the smooth running of the show and you'll find yourself listened to wisely. Do expect regular moodiness to manifest itself, though, especially if there's any hint of emotional tension in his or her home.

THE 2 EMPLOYEE

Just the person I'd want working for or with me: this is a naturally charming and affable human being who is diligent, co-operative and quickly learns to read your needs without being asked. Always make your 2 feel appreciated and let them know you're there for them too.

THE 2 LETTERS

B, K and T are all letters with the value and personality of 2. If your name carries many of these letters, or if your first name begins with one of these initials, you will have some particular 2 traits. Peaceable, friendly and co-operative, you will enjoy artistic pursuits in life and have a musical ear. You have an especially feminine side (which is no slur to all those sensitive Bens and Bruces) and women with these letters are especially maternal. If you are a 2 and lack one of these letters in your name, you may be prone to nervousness and self-doubt: indeed, all the more negative qualities of number 2.

THE 2 HOUSE

The perfect choice for a young married couple, this house is made for two to share and enjoy. It will be a peaceful home and friends will drop in for a fair hearing when they've quarrelled with their loved ones. It will be happiest decorated in subtle colours, but should have a splash of gold-pink or cinnamon shades to bring out its most harmonious spirit.

THE 2 PET

Your gentle pet is easy to live with, gets on with the milkman and the visiting in-laws, and loves to be stroked and petted. A naturally affectionate creature, they'll be a pleasure to share your life with, either in the house or the stable. Make sure you keep them away if you're feeling cranky and noisy.

WHAT HAPPENS IN A 2 YEAR?

A 2 year cycle will have been derived from the numbers of your birth day and month plus those of the current year adding up to 20: if they add up to 29 or 38 your year cycle is in fact a Master 11 year, so consult the penultimate chapter.

This is a year when you will be asked to think of those nearest to you in the most co-operative way possible. Some of your affairs are quite hard to read at the moment and you will need all your intuitive ability to see what's going on beneath the surface. Partnerships of all kinds come to the fore and you must listen to your inner voice about how to proceed with proposals and ideas put to you by these people.

On a business level, work progresses well and you will have offers of assistance from people around you. Be diplomatic with everyone to achieve your wishes and use tact when commenting on other people's ideas. Be prepared to bring together many disparate elements to make your dreams come true during this twelve-month period.

Love usually blossoms at this time, for 2 is the number of partnerships. It may be that a relationship which has been with you for some time suddenly clarifies, appearing stronger and more permanent. It may be that a proposal of marriage actually arises; at the very least, you will have a sense of knowing what you want from your current relationship and whether it is roadworthy for the many miles ahead of you. If you do begin this period without a love, this should definitely alter during the 2 cycle. Be gentle in persuading this lovely new soul to hang around for a while.

A 2 year brings up concerns with women. Perhaps you will find a strong new female friendship which has a lasting impact, or a new woman may enter your family life. You should also be able to trust women well in the area of business, or find a clever woman advises you on a particular course for your future. Either way, listen well.

Personal relationships may strangely demand that you see two different sides to a problem – in a 2 year, there will always be two sides to everything. Nevertheless, remember your intuition and powers of diplomacy are at an all-time high now, so you should have what it takes to handle the situation. In the twelve months previously (in a 1 year cycle) you have had to take the initiative and set off on a new path; now, you need to look deeply into matters and be a little more reliant on other people.

Take your time during this year: be neither dominant nor aggressive, but watch for your cue from others. Gentle persuasion works better now than bombastic or pushy behaviour. Be on the lookout for the most peaceful conclusions to even the smallest events. Also, slow yourself down a touch after the great push of last year: find a quiet spot to calm down and have a rest, taking just the dog or your newly focused partner with you.

THREE

Number 3 entertains the world: this is the number with the gift of the gab, the power to imagine and create, a love of people and merriment, but also with a capacity to gossip.

If you are a 3, or if you share your house with one, there will be a lot of laughter in your life. Though 3s sometimes lack direction, they are nevertheless optimistic and warm-hearted. There may well be many jobs started around the home – but they may not always be finished. But 3s know how to live: the very number itself suggests the life force.

The letters C, L and U belong to 3 so, if this is your number, use a name with one of these letters in it to avoid too much anxiety about what others think of you, as well as to counteract a tendency to constant throat problems. Your astrological relative is Gemini (also a talker); your colours are rose, ruby and russet; your scents are jasmine (for sensuality), rose otto (for balance and creativity) and neroli (to counter indecisiveness and nurture the inner child).

Day Force 3

Remember that your Day Force number is taken from the day of whichever month you were born. Your Day Force is 3 if your birthdate is the 3rd, 12th, 21st or 30th of any month and it exerts an influence over each and every day of your life. This number determines that you react like a 3 in everyday situations, with friends, co-workers, lovers and others.

All 3 Birthdays

With 3 influencing you every day you are one of nature's charmers. With a good eye for colour, an ear for music and a true appreciation of beauty and aesthetics, you are talkative, playful, good-humoured and a born communicator. You love to chat in a friendly way with anybody, making friends easily wherever you go. Your communication skills affect your capacity to write, speak, sing and act, so many 3s are actors or frustrated thespians. Apart from drama, you are skilled in many directions artistically.

This is a Day Force number with sharp mental skills and you love to acquire new information. Think of the juggler as a good metaphor for 3s: your hands can be quite busy, yet you can still toss another subject up into the air. You are usually interested, and gifted, in more subjects than one, just like your corresponding astrological sign, Gemini.

Entertaining is one of your strengths and you manage to give even a coffee break a party feel: you come to life at any party. If you are the host, you will have chosen everything carefully, paying attention to colour, lighting and mood as much as to what you eat and which kindred souls should come. Your optimum wish is that everyone will leave feeling elated, their minds buzzing, so you choose friends and feast to arrive at that end. Your personal contribution goes way beyond the lovely food to the skilful juggler's job of keeping the conversation bubbling along, ensuring every guest feels special, is spoken to and is heard. No number is a better host.

Despite being a party animal, you will have few really good friends, but these are of both sexes, who are equally drawn to your lovely gentle humour, your amazing general knowledge and your unforced charm.

Somehow you have a subject to share with everybody, finding common ground with the most unlikely companions.

Your 3 day number ensures a reasonable amount of luck with money on a regular basis, whereas those with 3 as a total Birth Force number often have to discover how to attract luck with money over the course of their lives. For you, little flutters and dabbles will frequently pay off and, as you're not greedy, the amounts are always in good proportion, never risking too much, always making a little more than you ventured.

3s have a lovely childlike aspect to their character – never growing old themselves, always able to bring fresh enthusiasm to the little surprises in life. This also means that as a 3 you communicate with children as one of them and know how to win their hearts. Your greatest weakness arises, nevertheless, from this childlike inclination to rush into too many things, your ability to turn your hand to various tasks. You run the risk of being the dilettante rather than the specialist and of dividing your energies into too many outlets, never achieving a sufficient degree of focus on any one of them. Try to balance your energies more, finish the wonderful imaginative things you start and avoid the frustrations you run into when you over-extend yourself.

With a 3 Day Force, make sure you use a name in your daily life (i.e. the name people actually call you by) that includes the letters C, L or U to get all the best qualities in your number. Without one of these, you may feel no-one is really listening to you. Or, you may not be communicating openly with those who are closest to you, at least emotionally.

BIRTHDAY ON 3RD

If your Day Force 3 arises from a birthday on the 3rd, your ability as a writer should be particularly pronounced. You will be immensely energetic, which will help you to recover from sadness or illness fairly quickly, and you like to get on with things once they've been agreed. Your imagination is very vivid, so you relate stories in a highly amusing anecdotal fashion, enabling you to spin simple yarns into money-earning short stories, or talk entertainingly at public functions: there is no better best man or master of ceremonies. You love showbiz and you have a witty way of verbally interpreting plays and poetry. You also love to read and dabble in a few different languages (but often without perfecting any).

For your career, you need to work with people, speaking to them and enticing them to talk to you. You would make a great counsellor, teacher, lecturer or PR consultant. For similar reasons you are a good lawyer, actor or writer; work centred on theatre/film/TV would also be a natural choice – especially as it gives you a varied menu. Try to avoid the nine-to-five routine.

BIRTHDAY ON 12TH

If your 3 Day Force derives from a birthday on the 12th, you are especially capable in the visually artistic areas of number 3. Still gifted at writing and advertising, your skills with colour, line and image are highly developed. If coupled with the usual 3 dramatic interest, this would mean film would be your special medium. You also take extra care in the presentation of gifts, projects and venues for entertaining. You are the consummate party-thrower. Career options, as well as those above, include design.

On the debit side, yours is a more nervous variation of 3 and you must curb your impatience with others a little. If you have lots of intellectual stimulation you should be able to absorb these nervy impulses, but if you have another personal number of 7 you will surely be too analytical and take nothing as straightforward or simple. Learn to take some things on trust.

BIRTHDAY ON 21ST

Lead a life that brings you into contact with music and dance, for you have excellent rhythm. You need lots of affection, but are sometimes inclined to suffer an emotional rollercoaster ride, turning hot and cold in your reactions to things and people. This in turn can lead to depressions (always short-lived) and moodiness, so in a relationship your lover must be a good friend as well, who can step back and leave you alone without undue worry if you're grumpy.

You enjoy reading as well as writing and journalism often suits those with your birthday, as does work in education, writing, art or PR. You love art, knowing what may make a good investment, and as ever you make friends with everyone you work alongside. In fact, working alone is not a good idea for you, because bouncing your ideas off others leads you on to greater and greater creativity.

BIRTHDAY ON 30TH

At work you are amusing and lively, but you need lots of free rein for your projects, and you would be the most unhappy of all the variations of 3 Day Force if you felt too confined. Your self-expression and individuality are magnetic, but on a down day you are nervous, easily exhausted and indecisive. Work against this with any number of meditative ploys, or use of calming colour and scent, to gently recover your poise. You are sometimes especially stubborn in your ideas and will benefit from listening to the cheering advice of others.

Drama and creative writing come easily to you, though you are also interested in occult subjects. Money turns up in your life easily and you are generous to others. As well as the dramatic/theatrical possibilities, you would enjoy a career in music, teaching or social work. Like everyone with a 3 Day Force, you attract a party atmosphere around you wherever you work.

BIRTH FORCE 3

Your Birth Force, from the addition of your whole birthdate including month and complete year, is 3. This is the number you will grow into during your life; it may take several adult years of experience before you feel the full force and expression of this number, as distinct from the Day Force which influences your most apparent personality traits each day.

With 3 as your Birth Force your main theme in life might be entertainment and self-expression. You love company and need the stimulus of groups to work at your best. When you are feeling positive, you will bask in the limelight and thrive on attention.

You will want and need to beautify your surroundings and seeing the results of your efforts will satisfy you. Your artistic eye is very sound and, though you will not strike out for anything too avant garde, you show originality and flair within the limits of what others might call good taste.

You can be proud at times, and also ambitious, impulsive and intolerant. Allow plenty of free rein to develop your sense of humour, as this is one of the best attributes given you to entertain and divert others. Over the course of your lifetime, your humour will also help you to learn how to offset a tendency to nervousness and lack of direction. Eventually, you will understand how to keep your skipping attention and high energy levels focused long enough to achieve your inspired goals.

It might be best to try to avoid a natural inclination to be a 'Jack of all trades' and hone your talents until you see a tangible outcome. Admittedly, if your work is too routine you will soon lose interest. Freedom is essential to your happiness and you would prefer to do anything rather than a strictly nine-to-five job. Nip your worrying tendencies in the bud, try to make the best of a situation, see the funny side of it and amuse others whilst you're about it. At intervals in your life you will recognise moments when you behave like a pair of clowns all by yourself: happy and sad, your moods may change from miserable to euphoric in seconds. But do remember you are a clown and humour is your best restorative. You will always feel you have achieved good results when you've turned a room full of forlorn faces into an office party.

All 3s are quite lucky with money: something to remember when the emotional rollercoaster takes you down for a spell. You are also creative and have the knack of inspiration at your fingertips. Working to an audience will be your best chance of happiness, or organising professional parties, functions, PR, designing, decorating, writing or beauty work. You are, of course, like a 3 Day Force, also an excellent teacher or lecturer, talker or actor.

Make sure you use a name with the letters C, L or U in it to make the best use of your energy and popularity, and to keep you lucky with money and friends.

This number is so connected with beauty that most of you will be blessed with good looks – and female 3s, very beautiful indeed, with a womanly figure. You love dressing up and have a way with scarves and jewellery, expressing yourself through colour and line. Your appearance is never ordinary.

In love you need a partner who copes with your popularity, but you also expect a lot as well. You may sometimes swamp your lover and be disappointed with the apparently unequal return – so hold on to your sense of proportion and remember your gift of making many people happy.

YOUR 3 LOVER

You've fallen on your feet here: this is a wonderful, funny, imaginative lover who will keep you occupied throughout your relationship if you give him or her a free rein. Your 3 is emotional and artistic, generally optimistic and a great lover of the good things in life. This suggests your time together will be bouncy and up-beat.

Your 3 love has a certain style: a way with words, a delicious dry sense of humour and an interesting way of seeming to stay young forever. In fact, it may be partly the childlike quality of your 3 that so lifts your own spirits. You are touched by the magic of his or her vision, the sense that all things are possible and the idea that life is a playground to be enjoyed to the full. In some respects your 3 is not entirely practical, but that is no matter: they believe, trust and are somehow always favoured with luck in every sense.

No-one loves a party more than your 3: he or she can turn an ordinary sandwich lunch into a celebration; when in charge of a serious event, the sky's the limit. Every detail will be brighter and more colourful than your imagination could have supposed. A 3 will take care of the music, the food, the aesthetic, the entertainment, the fancy dress, the champagne and, as a bonus, there will always be an element of the unexpected as well.

Once a 3 has fallen for you, you'll find evidence of their affection everywhere. A 3 in love is always happy, funnier than ever, flirtatious with the whole world but only interested in you. (Remember that the naturally charming 3 is nice to everyone, but this is not usually a threat.) Your enamoured 3 wears flamboyant clothing and spends freely on new items for his or her wardrobe. You will be urged to find new restaurants and clubs for each rendezvous, for anything tried too often is quickly stale. The one problem you may have with your 3 is in actually making a decision: 3s juggle ideas to such an extent that a simple choice can prove impossible. You'll often need to take the lead and make the decisions.

As a lover, your 3 is inventive and warm. He or she will bring their cheeky sense of fun into the bedroom and should make you feel very relaxed and ready for anything. Though not as raunchy and physical as a 5, your 3 is nevertheless very sensual and loves trying imaginative ideas, so take the lead a little and explore new possibilities with confidence. Any fun will be applauded, so dress up, or find new venues, or snatch some passion in the great outdoors: your 3 is forever a teenager, remember.

A 3 partner will be a happy recipient of your gifts and probably a generous giver as well. When you're buying them personal presents, opt for fashion: they love dressing up and have very decided style. They are almost always physically beautiful (or handsome) and have an artistic eye in putting their clothes together, adding a dashing touch by way of an unusual scarf or other accessories. Your 3 love is naturally very magnetic and if you can hold on to him or her, you will enjoy many good years together, whatever life has to offer.

And the downside? Well, if your 3 is one of those rare negative types, he or she will find their energy easily scattered and have trouble with the execution of tasks. Great plans for what to do together will be spoiled through lack of organisation and he or she may be just too extravagant to enjoy any security in life. They may be moody, or have too many unfinished undertakings; this can take away all the pleasure from your time together. But perhaps the biggest problem you'll have with your 3 love is jealousy: your 3 is always popular, but if this gets out of hand they may not know where to draw the line between buoyant fun and serious philandering. For you, nothing could be more distressing.

THE 3 CHILD

Your 3 child will want to be, and generally is, the most popular kid on the block. A born actor, clever at mimicry, warm and affectionate, this child has a lovely humour from the earliest age. He or she is easy to dress, enjoying fashion and having a well-developed personal style from the beginning. This is also a child with the gift of the gab, holding court with adults from infancy.

A 3 child is able to talk others into anything. They have such charm and enthusiasm for life: who can resist their appeal? If a girl, she will be interested in beauty, hairstyles and manicures, even before becoming a teenager. If a boy, he will stand out amongst his friends for a strongly individualistic style which is nevertheless not eccentric, but shows flair. With a child of either sex you will have a young designer on your hands, with something to say about the colour and style of the whole house, not just their own room.

Discourage any negative traits early: the worst of these is a tendency to gossip about friends, or exaggeration of problems real and imagined. Your 3 child may also be too much of a talker but not enough of a doer, owing partly to a surfeit of talents, but this often results in a lack of direction and focus. He or she will also have really moody days and this should be handled with care to discourage it. For the most part, though, your 3 child is a ray of sunshine – generous, warm and creative.

The 3 Boss

A charmer! He or she can ask for anything, and somehow you'll do it. They are generous and warm, skilled in lots of different ways and popular with everyone. They understand the need to keep a feeling of ritzy good humour in the office and are great hosts at the office party. A bit indecisive, sometimes.

The 3 Employee

Very cheerful and easy to work with, your 3 employee keeps the office happy. They are flexible about their job description, attractively presented, great at PR, good on the phone... you want more?

The 3 Letters

A generous sprinkling of the letters C, L or U in your name will give you many of the 3 characteristics. Notably, a first name beginning with any of these letters bestows creative talent and the gift of speech upon you. If you're a 3, you should use a name with one of these letters in it to avoid the trait of not having enough focus to utilise your many talents. You have good means of self-expression and the use of such a letter in your name ensures you will attract an audience.

The 3 House

An ideal place from which to make money, for it is lucky and attracts people to it. This is a house made to party in. Your friends will always drop in and you will be the envy of all, as it seems always to be a happy place. It's a great house for communications, so would make a good address as a centre of any kind, or would also be a superb address for a beauty clinic or actors' studio.

The 3 Pet

This is a loving pet who likes to contribute actively to the life of the home and family. Whether dog or cat, hamster or horse, lamb or lion, this is an animal who will make you laugh and seem almost to talk to you. Ready in a jiffy for a walk, happy to help you entertain, your furry (or otherwise) friend will win prizes for good looks at the local pet show and even charm your boss if sitting beneath your work desk.

WHAT HAPPENS IN A 3 YEAR?

Calculate your current year cycle by adding the numbers of your own birthday and month to the year you are in now (without your birth year). If this adds up and then reduces back to 3, your year cycle from birthday to birthday is governed by this number for twelve months.

With a twelve-month cycle of 3 you can expect a year of profits and reward, celebrations and rejoicing. You are set to embark on a very happy and busy period, so much so that at the end of the year you may wonder where the time has gone, so deeply will you have been immersed in your projects and leisure time.

All that you have been working toward for some time seems now to promise to bear fruit. The last year or two will have been spent in putting your shoulder to the wheel, so this is the period of harvest. This is true whether concerning business or relationships. All measure of reward is determined by the strength of your endeavours, but if you have been diligent, focused and tolerant of others in the preceding period, you can now expect fulfilment of your dreams.

On the social side this is a year of invitation and celebration. It could suggest a whirlwind love affair resulting in engagement or even marriage; if this takes place under this cycle, all augurs well. Certainly you will be in the thick of it socially, your popularity at its greatest, your powers of attraction radiant and your chances of meeting many exciting and attractive new friends high. A new lover at this time is quite likely to be generous and romantic, arranging delightful little trips or sudden surprises.

If you have a partner already, this may be the moment of truth, when you both decide to take your feelings a step further to the commitment stage. You may get the first chance you have had in a long time to relax a little together and take a really exciting holiday. If you are in business together or work at the same place, promotion or success could be your deserved reward. Whatever is in the wind romantically will blossom; whatever business seeds you sow should become strong shoots in no time.

Your mind is alive and vital, you are clever and witty, you see things clearly. Any amount of artistic promise within you should thrive now, so much so that you surprise yourself with your own ability. Anything you spend time on in creative terms, whether a painting, a play, some writing, craft work, or music, will have a touch of brilliance in it. For this reason, and as ideas seem to come thick and fast now, you may work overtime trying to cram in all that you want to do.

You should find a new or stronger interest in philosophy or metaphysics seizes your imagination. You will communicate your theories brilliantly, especially to children. You might decide to write something for children or make a film or painting with younger people in mind. Suffice to say that your cognitive processes are firing, and your mind is in a superior state.

If you don't use this cycle well you could experience a delay in reward, or fail to listen to your own inner spark of motivation. But this number is so good that really nothing seems to dent its power very much. Bear in mind that this is a fertile cycle, in every way, and that you must watch out for pregnancies if they are not yet wanted.

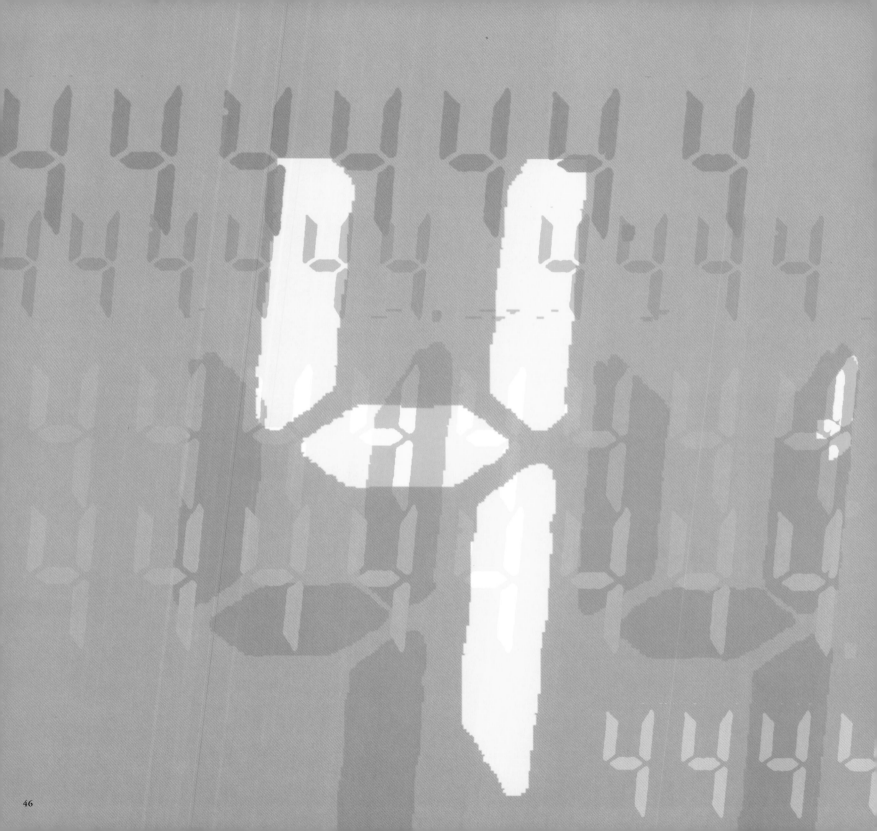

FOUR

THIS IS THE NUMBER OF CAREFUL PLANS AND APPLICATION. STEADY AS A ROCK, 4 IS THE NUMBER OF FOUNDATIONS WELL LAID, FOUR-SQUARE, AND ALSO OF THE FAMILY UNIT. GREATER EVEN THAN 2 AT CHECKING DETAILS, 4 IS METHODICAL, SERIOUS AND CONSERVATIVE, BUT CAN SOMETIMES LACK A FREE IMAGINATION.

IF YOU ARE A 4, OR YOU LIVE WITH ONE, TASKS AROUND YOUR HOME WILL BE PROPERLY THOUGHT OUT, PLANNED FOR AND FINISHED. LIFE IS USUALLY VERY ORDERLY: PAPERS FILED, SURFACES CLEANED, CUPBOARDS NEAT AND WELL STOCKED. A 4'S HANDBAG OR GLOVE-BOX CONTAINS THE ESSENTIALS FOR AN EMERGENCY. BUT MATTERS PROGRESS SLOWLY AND CAREFULLY, INSTEAD OF GREAT CHANGES SWEEPING THROUGH ON A REGULAR BASIS.

YOUR LETTERS — D, M AND V — ENSURE THAT YOU USE YOUR SENSE OF ORDER CONSTRUCTIVELY: WITHOUT THESE LETTERS IN THE NAME YOU USE, YOU MAY FEEL YOU CAN NEVER GET THINGS TO RUN SUFFICIENTLY SMOOTHLY AND THAT YOUR BUDGET IS IMPOSSIBLE TO CONTROL. IF YOU ARE A 4 BUT LACK ANY OF THESE LETTERS, YOU MAY BE CRITICISED FOR EXTREME SERIOUSNESS AND LACK OF FLEXIBILITY, OR YOUR FAMILY LIFE MAY BE RATHER UNSTABLE. YOUR COLOURS — GREEN, BLUE, AND INDIGO — WILL BRING YOU LUCK; YOUR SCENTS ARE CITRUS (GRAPEFRUIT AND LIME), BERGAMOT (AGAINST EXHAUSTION AND MENTAL PRESSURE) AND GINGER (BOOSTS FORTITUDE AND CONFIDENCE); YOU ARE RELATED TO THE STAR SIGN CANCER.

DAY FORCE 4

Your Day Force number is taken from the day of whichever month you were born and determines that in everyday situations and in frequent reaction to situations that arise with friends, co-workers, lovers and other circumstances, you react with the character traits of your number. Your Day Force is 4 if your birthdate is the 4th, 13th or 31st of any month. However, if your birthday is the 22nd, you are a Master Number 22 rather than a 4 which, like 11, is never reduced. Turn to the last chapter to read about 22, but you might be interested to read about 4s and notice the overlap as well as the subtle differences.

ALL 4 BIRTHDAYS

You often get a bad press for being the sensible, hard-working one. You might be thought of as the embodiment of the dictum regarding 'all work and no play' making you sometimes dull, but this is unfair. Though a very negative 4 may show signs of extreme seriousness or an obsession with detail at the cost of the greater picture, the majority of 4s are the most dependable of all numbers, with great powers of concentration and a real knack for finding the method with which to attack, and attain, the greatest heights.

You are a keyholder to the ideas and creative urges of other numbers: you know better than anyone how to make a dream into a reality. Almost certainly you are quite mathematical, good at DIY and clever with your hands. 4s are the builders on the planet, creating the cornerstone for others' flights of fancy.

Yours is a rational number, but not without its spiritual dimension. Notably, though, philosophical musings must be sensible ideas, easy to grasp and to explain, for them to appeal to you. And your artistic merits are built on solid blocks: many 4s are very musical (perhaps connected with a facility for maths) and they have the patience to train hard, and practise well, at a chosen skill. Thus, 4s often achieve a destiny in music, or even stage and theatre, because of their very solidity, while other more flamboyant and obviously arty people have no follow through and dream, only, of their goal.

Your number is connected with the earth, so you may well be green-fingered and love your garden. Even if a small patio is all you have to play with, you are delighted to get your hands dirty and grow something. Given space, yours will be the best vegetable garden, or herb patch, because these plants have both an aesthetic and a practical use. You like things that are real, that you can hold onto; you have the perseverance to encourage tiny seedlings to become healthy little plants – even metaphorically.

Be not alarmed that you are not the originator of ideas, but you are the one to get them done, making you the best employee, the hardest worker in any organisation. You always need order around you to function well; an untidy room or desk will seriously impede you. You arrange a system which others are happy to copy and you also have a reputation for honesty and straightforward speech. You will say what you think and be counted on for your common-sense appraisal. You may well have a constant stream of hard knocks and sharp falls, but you have the mettle to pick yourself up and go on. Your courage is witnessed by all who know you.

Try to be aware that your opinions are possibly too fixed, and to listen to all options before you select a method for progress. Your other difficulty comes from being so intent on detail that you are slow off the mark; though, admittedly, this can be a classic illustration of the hare and the tortoise in action.

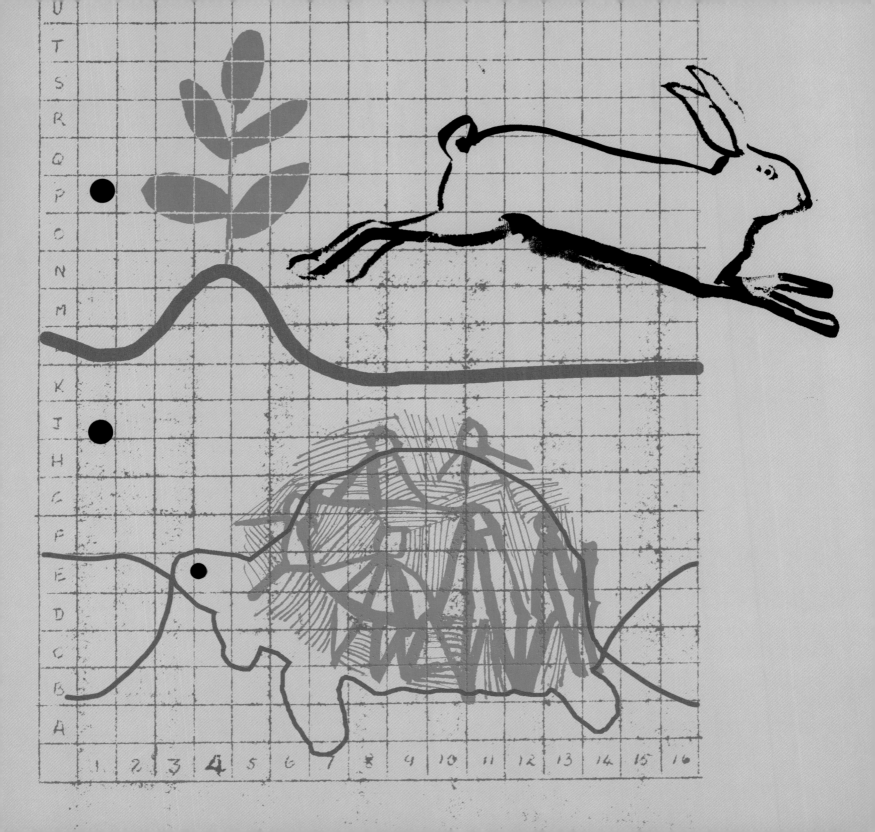

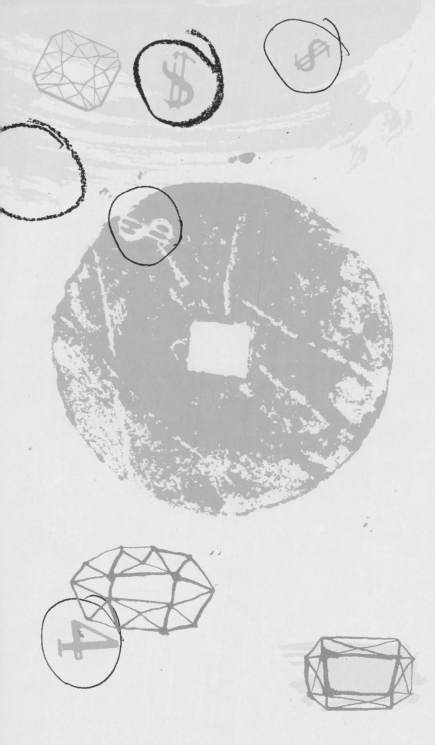

BIRTHDAY ON 4TH

A birthday on the 4th of any month suggests you are a hard-working and apparently well organised person with a natural ability in business. You can be the most economical and conscientious of the numbers; a job left to you for completion will be in safe hands, no matter how banal it may seem to others. You are practical, laying solid foundations to build up your world. Your honesty and forthrightness ensure success in all you do.

Loyalty is a powerful characteristic, for which you gain respect every day of your life in little ways. You are also very emotional, in spite of your seeming caution about life; however, you may be disinclined to show this because of your practical and careful nature and subsequently receive few of the overt tokens of love which you crave as much as other people. Never let it be said that you are unromantic – but you may have to learn to unleash this part of you so that others may also come to realise it.

You are an indefatigable worker when inspired, enabling you to drive others as well as yourself to finish a job within a deadline. What you must watch is the possibility of driving yourself too hard and allowing your health to suffer as a consequence. Remember to incorporate your oils (bergamot especially) to combat stress and exhaustion.

4s are good workers whatever they do. But because your birthday is the pure 4, your natural inclination might be towards building and architecture and all things connected with it, as well as any work requiring careful concentration or use of the hands. Business, banking, clerical work, accountancy, drafting and design, writing, managing, statistical work, hard-graft secretarial (such as a personal assistant whose job is largely to organise someone else) or businesses connected with property or insurance are obvious outlets for your skills.

Your negative traits are a real stubbornness and a tendency to be too set in your ways. Some might think you are too blunt in the way you express yourself, but this stems from a basic need for directness. You dislike change, being on the conservative side, and you feel you must try something out for yourself before you will give it credence.

BIRTHDAY ON 13TH

People fear that the 13th is an unlucky birthday. This is not really so, but the number is nevertheless often misunderstood and given a bad press (it is, of course, the witches' number, for there are thirteen moons in the year they work by). If you are born on this day you may have decided that you have to work especially hard for the things that really matter to you and this is often true. But you have a wonderful ability in managerial and detailed work, as well as a better understanding of other people's suffering than any other 4 birthday.

You are entirely loyal and honest, accurate in work demanding great concentration, with a driving ambition. You work hard and drive others to the same performance. You will succeed best if your home is stable and family life strong and supportive. In fact, 13s need security very badly, and you may go to great lengths to achieve this. You can be terribly stubborn, hard to shake off a course when you have set your mind to it, no matter how hopeless that course may seem. You can be dictatorial, too, and relentlessly unforgiving if someone offends you really deeply.

You are very sensitive and may truly suffer if you feel oppressed by a restricted environment. You are strongly loving and actually very sensuous – more so than any other 4 – but may be frightened to demonstrate this. You will get into difficulty as a result of being misunderstood, even by those who believe they know you well. You can be temperamental, but you are also inspirational and powerful if your forcefulness is well directed. As 13 is the witches' number, it bestows great psychic and intuitive gifts and an excellent facility for seeing the whole picture, rather than just the minutiae of details which often bog other 4s down. Yours is the number of wisdom from experience: use your knowledge.

Workwise, you belong in the business world. You have the basic organisational abilities of all the 4s and would thrive in (and enjoy) accountancy, building, property, architecture, merchandising, buying and working with wood, gems or minerals. Also, like the other 4s, you have a talent for writing, and would be especially good at journalism or writing reports, both of which require practical slog as well as mental concentration.

BIRTHDAY ON 31ST

This is the best 4 birthday for business and organisation. With this Day Force you will usually be long-lived, a practical achiever and a hard worker. You will always repay kindnesses and have a long memory for people who have helped you. Try to keep your aspirations within reach to avoid inescapable disappointments.

You are very loyal to any cause you take to heart, as well as to family and friends. You are dominant, determined and will exert tremendous efforts to achieve your desired end. You will enjoy travel, but also love returning home. You should not live alone, as family and close friends form an important part of your support network. You will be very well suited to marriage or responsible relationships.

You can be very thrifty and honest, feeling happier if your accounts are in good order. If your environment is well arranged you will function more efficiently, but you will resent anyone's interference in your methods. You can be extremely stubborn.

Health and its associated subjects will be of interest to you. You may be acutely aware of diet and hygiene, and you will have a logical understanding of drugs and herbals, cures and first aid procedures. Many people with this birthday choose medicine as a career. You would also succeed in the area of building and property, contracting, accountancy, writing, clerical and book work, illustrating and health foods.

Your worst flaw is probably a confused reaction to change and an inclination to obsessive precision. Friends may not know how to cope with this. If you've had a particularly conventional upbringing, you may also be very serious indeed and unable to laugh at yourself if things go awry. Don't let this prevent you from using your tremendous strength to start again if need be and have the last laugh on those who doubted the wisdom of your path.

Birth Force 4

You Birth Force is 4 if the total number of your whole birthday – day, month and year – can be reduced to 4 (unless it totals 22, when you are a Master Number 22 and should turn to the last chapter). Your Birth Force is the number you grow into across the course of your life, whereas the Day Force is apparent daily in your immediate reactions.

With a Birth Force of 4, your lifetime's achievement will be the careful management of your own and others' affairs, especially in business, and construction in the material sense (governing building and execution of design) and the metaphorical sense. You learn to be the doer, rather than the talker, understanding how to ensure that ideas are actualised.

Over the years you will acquire a great degree of rational thought and exposition; you find ways to arrange and maintain a system for achieving well in life. Your gift is to see quickly the practical route through obstacles that besiege others' dreamy but interesting ideas. To you it is obvious how to attain tangible results in all things. You have a brilliant approach to the use of time and know, instinctively it seems, what projects to invest time in, because these are the ones that will come to fruition. Where a 1 will conceive an idea and verbalise it to others, a 2 will choose the team for execution and find out what is involved and a 3 will add glamour and the vision of how the project may look, beautifying it along the way, it is for the 4 actually to find the materials and the workable plans by which the thing can be built, or realised. All the others do the thinking: you do the work.

You are progressively dissatisfied with mere ideas: your urge is to make things real or forget them. With enviable perseverance and determination, you see the true possibility within a project if any exists and then unfold the manner in which to make the lasting form. You get things done and also keep a tidy path as you move towards fulfillment of the task. Any inquisitive accountant will find you an easy person to work with, for your paperwork is tidy and your thoughts clear. You are not the one to waste time building castles in the air: you look for a good site and the right building stone. You attend to the details, where most other numbers see only an overall picture

of the desired end. This makes you a stickler, in many ways, or what some people call a party-pooper – for you put paid to any schemes which are likely to remain only a fantasy. Your greatest talent, perhaps, is that of being able to differentiate between what is a wild idea and what has real merit.

You have a very high standard of honour. You prefer to work steadily, and like to see others apply the same industry. You don't take chances with money, or gamble: that is for a 5. You manage your money and make it work for you. You have a systematic approach and often create order without noticing that you do so. You are happy to assist others, but scornful of those who get themselves into constant hot water, either emotionally or financially. Yours is the real world: why do other people live in the clouds?

Your willingness to work hard suggests many careers and you may dip into several of them. Your rational mind is at ease with the sciences, technology and mathematics. Your eye for detail is also suited to investigative work, which would include research and journalism. Property is the other area for your skills: real estate, working and managing the land, or anything connected with building. Slow, steady work is the key to your success. If your Day Force provides your career, you will nevertheless find that at least a leisure interest in these areas is inescapable. Wear green and blue in business to keep you focused and content.

In love, you are likely to find happiness with someone who loves simple pleasures, the home and garden, and a secure business and financial life. You are loyal and not likely to keep searching for the perfect dream, but settle down to the hard work of daily relationships. But you must guard against a flat and unromantic manner: there will always be days that require a little mystery and extra care – try to be imaginative as well.

YOUR 4 LOVER

Presumably you are attracted to your 4 because of his or her steadiness and dependability. It may be that you feel secure in the arms of this down-to-earth soul, whose humour is dry and sometimes unconscious and who delivers (almost always) exactly what they promise. Assuredly you are not expecting a lover who will bring you flowers or book passionate impromptu holidays in exotic locations! Your 4 is made of sensible stuff and you will get a better reaction if you are thrilled to bits with a new kitchen than if you hope for designer clothes and Belgian chocolates.

Your 4 enjoys a date at a restaurant that is good value and has the added bonus of being just down the road. Time spent getting there is time wasted, and your 4 will definitely prefer not to have to get too dressed up for any venue. Very clean but comfortable sporty clothes are his or her choice; when you are choosing fashion gifts for this partner, check that they are hard-wearing and don't need dry cleaning to keep them in top condition. Your beloved likes clothes that give long wear and good service, but being able to keep them neat and conservatively appealing is a priority. Once your 4 has really made it financially (which is a sound bet), tailor-made clothes are a real possibility.

Your 4 love has strong opinions and a decided moral code by which to live. He or she is as honest as they come and expects the same from you. If you stray, or flirt, you are unlikely to be easily forgiven. Once a 4 has made up their mind to a course of behaviour, nothing can shake them.

And, of course, a flighty lover – however appealing in other ways – is not the one to marry. Your 4 is investing in you for your reliability and capacity to stay the course. You must be as calm in a crisis, as ordered in your daily life, as unlikely to be overdrawn at the bank as they are themselves.

A 4 love also has much to offer. Here is a companion who will work hard to make your home and family life run well, with plenty of money, a well-designed and healthy space to live in and a job which gives them pleasure as well as reward. A 4 is too practical to put up with anything less than what is comfortable and sensible. Your 4 also runs your house with skill and seemingly effortless control.

Despite the reputation 4s have for a lack of imagination, your 4 love is quite likely to be more creative than you think. All 4s are incredibly clever with their hands, be it art, music, creative work or DIY. I have known many 4 women who were formidable with power tools, while their brilliant and creative husbands stood by watching, amazed, as taps were changed, plumbing finished, roof tiled, doors hinged.

Always tell your 4 what is bothering you: they admire, even demand, your honesty and will generally react evenly to what you say. Sometimes you will want to ask for more cuddles, or a romantic dinner (blow the expense) once in a while. It is not that they will refuse: just that they didn't think of it. And, as you grow old together, you can look forward to more security and loyal love than almost any of your friends. This is one to keep – if you can get past the early, rather unromantic stages.

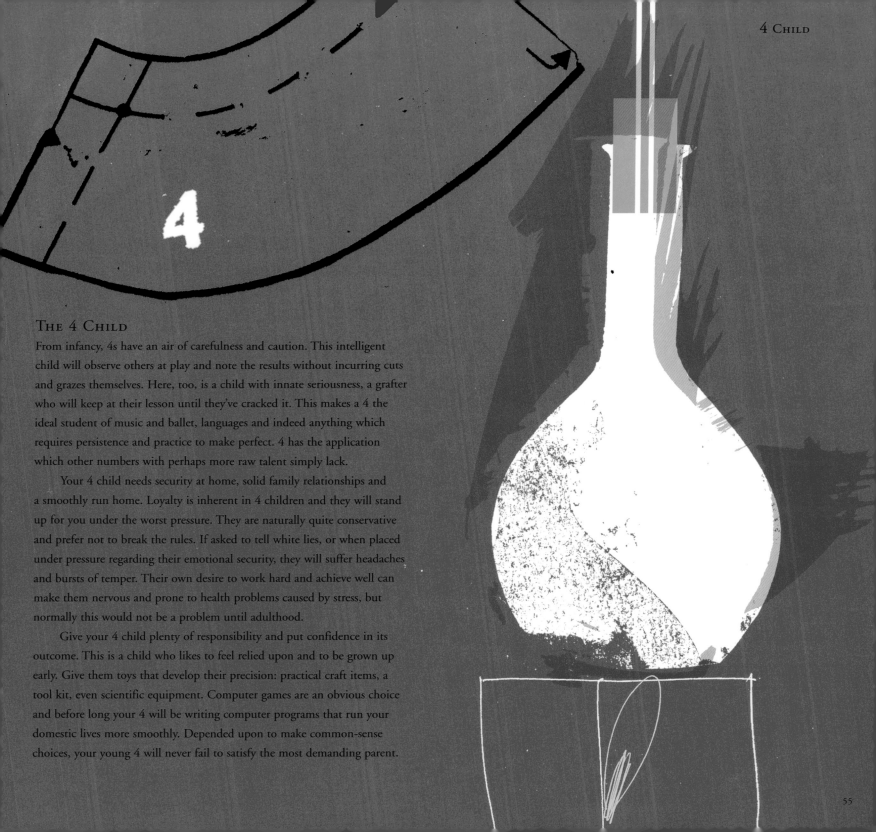

THE 4 CHILD

From infancy, 4s have an air of carefulness and caution. This intelligent child will observe others at play and note the results without incurring cuts and grazes themselves. Here, too, is a child with innate seriousness, a grafter who will keep at their lesson until they've cracked it. This makes a 4 the ideal student of music and ballet, languages and indeed anything which requires persistence and practice to make perfect. 4 has the application which other numbers with perhaps more raw talent simply lack.

Your 4 child needs security at home, solid family relationships and a smoothly run home. Loyalty is inherent in 4 children and they will stand up for you under the worst pressure. They are naturally quite conservative and prefer not to break the rules. If asked to tell white lies, or when placed under pressure regarding their emotional security, they will suffer headaches and bursts of temper. Their own desire to work hard and achieve well can make them nervous and prone to health problems caused by stress, but normally this would not be a problem until adulthood.

Give your 4 child plenty of responsibility and put confidence in its outcome. This is a child who likes to feel relied upon and to be grown up early. Give them toys that develop their precision: practical craft items, a tool kit, even scientific equipment. Computer games are an obvious choice and before long your 4 will be writing computer programs that run your domestic lives more smoothly. Depended upon to make common-sense choices, your young 4 will never fail to satisfy the most demanding parent.

The 4 Boss

Cautious, solid, demanding high skills and great diligence from you, this boss is less likely to harass you about wearing skimpy clothing or gaze down your neck-line than worry that your expenses are in order and your paperwork filed. This is someone who is something of a perfectionist, likes getting the job done on time and under budget; but they will show solid, if not playful, appreciation. Don't take too many sick days.

The 4 Employee

The perfect choice: while everyone else is still at lunch, a 4 will be happily clearing their desk so they can move on to the next thing. Loyal, honest and reliable about checking all the requirements, here is someone you will be happy to have working for you for years. And if you need a sudden computer servicer or software expert, there's your man (or woman).

The 4 Letters

If you are a 4, use a name which incorporates one of the letters D, M or V to make full use of your practical strengths. The letter D, particularly, helps to anchor you and give you a sense of the personal security you need, while M bestows the emotional strength to shoulder all the burdens life thrusts upon you. If your name begins with one of these letters, whatever your birthday, you too will take on some of the properties of that number 4. D and M give you steadiness and logical thought, a love of home and security, and probably a position of authority gained from your reliability. V makes you stubborn and either very practical or very impractical.

The 4 House

Clearly the best number for a family home. This house will lend itself to secure family life, not too many leaks or bumps in the night and should represent a solid if not meteoric investment. Most 4 homes also have wonderful (even when tiny) gardens and attract buyers who enjoy keeping them neat and tidy, even if their taste is safe rather than cutting-edge.

The 4 Pet

Perversely, while number 4 is consistently associated with hard work, a 4 pet is likely to be lazy. They will never do more than is absolutely required of them and this could mean just dozing by the fire. However, your 4 pet may also be a gardener (watch those holes), a hunter and an excellent watchdog (even the budgie). They will do all this in the name of practicality; but this creature is happiest just being securely and loyally by your side, at home – in fact, the ideal family pet.

WHAT HAPPENS IN A 4 YEAR?

You will know by now that the number governing any given year is arrived at by adding the numbers of your birthday and month to the year that you are currently in, instead of your year of birth. Thus, each year your temporary cycle moves on by one number in nine-year cycles.

A twelve-month cycle adding up to the number 4 is a challenge. It is traditionally characterised by hard work, a need for detail and perhaps some attention to your domestic security and property. Often, too, this is the moment in which your finances come under inspection and you must work to put yourself on solid ground.

Be tactful with others; you will have to fit in with their needs as best you can. You are full of energy and motivation, which could bring about extraordinary accomplishment if well directed. But there is equally a chance of offending others and causing dissent if you do not watch your tongue: people will misinterpret your aggression and determination and become quarrelsome, which you must try to avoid. Otherwise you may spend much of this year feeling isolated and misunderstood.

If you can harness your positive attitude, new opportunities will arise in business and you can look forward to changes for the better. This could be an ideal time for financial speculation, even though 4 is normally a careful number, as everything seems to combine for success; but do not allow your affairs to be dogged by disorganisation, which is a major concern for the number 4. To win, you must become systematic in all you do.

There is every chance that you will be 'noticed' to your advantage during this time. You will have a showcase to demonstrate your worth, which is great for business; but also, you will either attract many admirers (or one special one), or find that somebody who can really alter the shape of your future life appears and begins to inspire you.

During this time, your talents may be given a free rein. This will be especially true if you are trying to break into film or television or some other arts-related field, but it could be just as fitting in any business environment. Once you have your chance, your capacity for hard work and your good memory will serve to keep you there. Moreover, under a 4 vibration, nothing goes to your head: your feet are firmly on the ground and you have what it takes to work fixedly.

Legal elements sometimes materialise under this number cycle, so don't allow any documents which need your attention to be put aside. You must apply yourself to the task calmly and practically, and in the event that you must deal with something weightier – such as house deeds (very possible), claims of any kind or settlements from the past – try to be as co-operative as possible. You will lose out if you let pride or greed govern your actions, as honesty and fairness are essential under the number 4.

The onus is on you during this entire cycle to look for ways of working with those around you, whether this is in business or in your personal relationships. Try to be as reasonable as you can and find the common ground for resolving differences of opinion. If you do this you can certainly expect excellent fortune in material terms and also the resolution of matters of the heart that have confused or frustrated you.

Regimentalise your daily life under this number; you will thrive from doing so. A 4 cycle is usually demanding workwise, so you may only achieve all that's required of you by carrying out your plans in an extremely methodical way. Get your house in order, too, for this is the optimum time to fix broken bits, lay the foundations for a good garden or simply convert leftover space so that your home underscores your wish for security.

FIVE

NOW WE REACH THE CHAPTER OF PROGRESS: THIS NUMBER IS, FIRST AND FOREMOST, CONCERNED WITH CHANGE. THE FIRST FOUR NUMBERS CONCEIVE, FLESH OUT AND THEN SYSTEMATICALLY EXECUTE IDEAS, WITH NUMBER 4 REPRESENTING THE CONSERVATIVE, CAREFUL ACHIEVEMENT AND CONSOLIDATION OF PLANS. NOW NUMBER FIVE CHANGES DIRECTION AND USHERS IN A NEW LIFE FORCE AND ENERGY.

THIS, THEN, IS THE NUMBER OF TRAVEL, EXCITEMENT, A NEW LEASE OF LIFE. 5S ARE FOREVER YOUNG, SPEAK PERSUASIVELY AND INSIST (EVEN GENTLY) ON REVOLUTION. THIS IS THE ACTIVE NUMBER SEXUALLY; PHYSICALLY IT IS ALWAYS IN MOTION. WATCH A 5 ON THE TELEPHONE AND NOTICE THAT THEY CAN'T SIT STILL. ALWAYS PERIPATETIC, 5S CAN ONLY THINK WHEN THEY'RE ON THEIR FEET. WITH A BAG FULL OF TALENTS, 5S WILL EITHER INSPIRE YOUR ADMIRATION OR DRIVE YOU TO NERVOUS EXHAUSTION. A 5 IN THE HOUSE KEEPS THE LAUGHTER LEVEL HIGH – PASSIONS, TOO. A 5 YEAR CYCLE WILL CERTAINLY MEAN A CHANGE OF PACE AND PROBABLY A TRIP.

THE LETTERS E, N AND W ALL HAVE THE PROPERTIES OF NUMBER 5; THE COLOURS CONNECTED WITH THIS NUMBER ARE CHERRY, RASPBERRY, LAVENDER AND WISTERIA. THE SCENTS OF 5 ARE LAVENDER (FOR CALMING), SANDALWOOD (FOR NERVOUS STRAIN) AND PEPPERMINT (FOR ENERGY). YOUR ASTROLOGICAL EQUIVALENT IS LEO.

DAY FORCE 5

Your Day Force, as you know, is the date of the month in which you were born, reduced to a single digit. You have a Day Force of 5 if you were born on the 5th, 14th or 23rd of any month. All the 5s have many properties in common, but your particular birthday gives a slightly different spin on the number, so those born on the 5th are a little different from those on the 14th, and so on.

ALL 5 BIRTHDAYS

All 5 Day Force numbers will bestow great originality and dynamism on their holders. Versatility and mental elasticity go with the number, so all 5s stay well-informed, have many strings to their bow, and enjoy the freedom with which to pursue all their interests. Freedom, indeed, is as basic a requirement to a 5's survival as air. If you're a 5 Day Force, you need flexibility in your daily life, and the security and order which a 4 craves are positively deathly to you.

With a 5 Day Force you are the verbalist par excellence of all the numbers. You are gifted at languages, have a lovely wit and show great charm whenever it is needed. You perceive someone in trouble when they cannot articulate a grievance or idea and you subtly take their part, presenting a cogent case which wins the day. You feel a duty to the public, often just to be spokesperson; your natural curiosity insists that you uncover all the information pertaining to any situation. This makes you a great debater, and an amusing one too.

You have no fears about pushing out into the world. Rushing in where angels fear to tread is a weekly pursuit for you. You know no bounds; you enjoy pushing the frontiers of the known world. You are all for inventions to improve existing life and exploration to increase current knowledge. You are also progressive in your ideas, enjoying freedom of mind and body yourself and acknowledging this basic right for all. Sometimes this suggests a liberality bordering on hedonism, for you throw off restraint of any kind.

Sexually, you have your own moral code; with your number being as physical as it is, you are likely to enjoy the pleasures of a sensual life as much as anyone can. 'Wine, women and song' – with suitable gender inversions as applicable – might well be your catchphrase.

Every day of your life you must find a way to achieve variety. Routine would deaden your lively mind; too great a demand for logic would deny you your exciting ability to make the impossible dream perfectly accessible. You like to gamble a little, inspiring such confidence in others that your whims nearly always pay off. You also need travel, a change of scene and engagement with different cultural ideas to bring out the best in you. You are an entertainer, pure and simple: as such, you must be given your stage.

Fight the restlessness, often at the expense of all you've gained, which is one of the negative traits of your number. So, too, is a capacity for nervous energy and a sense of dissatisfaction with life. With all your abilities, you must be careful not to have too many irons in the fire, none of which you hone properly.

Remember that a good education, and proper training according to your field, is vital to help you realise your exceptional mental agility. If you lack this you may be over-hasty in your efforts, or have outbursts of temper, or simply be undisciplined in your life. This is caused by frustration: you must try to curb impatience as best you can and apply your clever mind to learning.

5555   55555555555   55555555555   5

BIRTHDAY ON 5TH

With pure 5 as a Day Force you are both intellectual, versatile and have
an investigative nature. You are a very physical person, full of energy and
restlessness, and you will be extremely attractive to (and popular with) the
opposite sex. With your magnetic personality and clever tongue you would
be an excellent salesperson, and your enthusiasm is contagious. No-one can
refuse you.

Invest in good-quality luggage as yours is the most obvious birthday for
travel (together with those born on the 9th). You love life, new experiences
and changes, so should never be too tightly tied down. You should be
confident in following your hunches as you have a gambler's instinct. Unless
you find a love partner with a like free-minded disposition, you will forever
be trying to break free – no matter how strong the sexual magnetism that
drew you together.

Your best career options are in any field which puts you before the
public and gives you a chance to move around. Editor, analyst, traveller
or writer are all roles you could play; you would also succeed in real estate,
public speaking or insurance. You have the pioneer spirit and are a progressive
thinker; variety must be the spice of your life.

Birthday on 14th

This points to a constructive or destructive power, depending on how it is handled. With this number you will be very physical, with stronger spiritual aspirations than the other 5s, loving change and variety, and relishing travel and freedom as the other 5s all do. You are extremely magnetic and saucy – more of a law-breaker than other 5s – and you show immense versatility in getting on with just about anybody.

You have two distinct sides to your personality and you have both a reasoning and prophetic mind. On a good day you can be charming and silver-tongued; on a bad day, very sharp in your speech. You show the quickness of thought characteristic of all 5s, but you also have an impulsive streak that could perhaps be curtailed at times. You will be interested in everything new and, like the sign Aquarius (which is actually the opposite of your corresponding astrological sign, Leo), you will be delighted to try out the most modern gadgetry and be up-to-date with the current thinking. You will take a chance on most things and have the 5's gambling instinct; but beware, this may get out of hand if given a chance.

Try not to become involved in relationships for reasons of pure physical attraction; or, if you do so, don't entertain false hopes as to where these relationships might lead. You can be an idealist about love, but sometimes the surface does not match the content. You are emotional, though, so can be reached through your feelings. A steady, loving relationship would be your best chance of stability and might dissuade you from being too flippant or fickle.

Business may suit you better than artistic work, the more so as you would excel in any business of your own. Manage your own affairs for optimum success, but be wary of over-indulgence in either drink or sex. The best lines of business for you are in buying and selling, travelling, promotional work, tours, brokerage, property or journalism – this last because of the variety it offers. If an artistic path does interest you, choose something which leaves you time to replenish any nervous energy you expend. Thus, music may be better and more calming than acting; or painting may be less stressful than fashion design, though you will be skilled in several of these directions. At all costs, do not get yourself into a work situation where your freedom is jeopardised or your ideas limited.

Birthday on 23rd

With the 2 in front of the 3, you are used to giving other people's needs a high priority. You ought to follow a profession, but if you do choose to work in the business world you will bring professionalism to it. You are practical and intellectual, quick-witted and energetic and, like a good lawyer, you have the ability to think on your feet. Ready and willing to accept sudden change, you adapt to new people and environments with relish, and you are a keen traveller who will notch up many miles. In fact, travel is likely to play a regular role in your affairs, even as part of your job.

People find you charismatic and charming; in particular, you deal extremely well with the opposite sex, who will be of much assistance to you throughout your life. You will be an achiever, perhaps more so than any 5; you should aim high so that you feel proud of what you create. You have a nervous energy and an impulsiveness which may get you into trouble sometimes, but no-one stays angry with you for long. You are, after all, very generous, as well as highly motivated, and you know how to inspire others when they are down. You are like a vitamin pill or tonic that gets others on their feet again after a bad spell.

You are a very physical, sensual person: sexually, you know exactly what you want, and you are adventurous and mischievous. But you will need a partner who is of a like spirit and mind, who does not feel threatened by you. Your love must be your playfellow, with a great sense of humour and a sense of daring, too.

You often gamble with people or in a situation, and you have a promoter's instincts for what will be appealing to others. You can talk anyone into almost anything. Most important of all to you, perhaps, is that you must be given your freedom, whether at work or in relationships, to do things your own way. You could not be idle for too long.

Workwise, people with this number enjoy any position offering scope for self-motivation, travel and activity. It is an excellent birthday for the film business, and there's bound to be something of the actor or producer in you (Shakespeare's birthday was reputedly 23rd April). It is also the number for teaching and writing, professional travelling, sales and advertising. Whatever you may do under this Day Force number, it is certain that life won't be dull.

BIRTH FORCE 5

Your Birth Force differs from your Day Force, not only in that it is derived from all the numbers of your birthday (date plus month plus birth year) but also in that it takes many years for its influence to be felt. Where your Day Force is apparent in your character and daily reactions, the characteristics of your Birth Force develop over a lifetime's experience. Across your life, the number 5 will eventually explain the deepest facets of your nature.

Your Birth Force (also called Life Lesson) number of 5 means that, over the years, you will not only call for but initiate change within your family, community and society. With this number you have an overall need for freedom and a desire for variety, a horror of being stuck in a rut for years on end. Your enthusiasm for any project will strain at the leash if you feel limited, so ideally you should be in a position where travel and movement are part of your overall lifestyle. You need to aim towards, and grow into, challenging situations from which you can learn, as your mind needs to be constantly stretched in different ways.

Because 5 is a very physical number and highly sexed, you will discover how to enjoy your own physicality and eventually understand your needs and desires in the sensual, physical world. This means a relationship which does not provide an ongoing sexuality for you will ultimately not fulfil your needs; you must be active and you need passion in your life. Without it, your lovely sense of humour and vitality will atrophy.

You will also become a good talker, an avid reader and a witty conversationalist. You acquire an instinct in situations of chance, but must try not to overdo this as it could become an obsession. You become progressively independent and less inclined, therefore, to take others' advice; but your natural affability will get you out of most tight situations.

You need to have several outlets for your talents, and it is quite possible that you will run two businesses parallel to each other. One may be your best source of livelihood, whilst the other is a talent that pays on the side. Probably, you will find that you become restless if you are stuck in a groove for too long, but you should learn eventually how to use your amazing resourcefulness to keep things moving and find new corners of interest within any given field.

You will travel a good deal; as a corollary interest you may learn languages quickly and well, and come to appreciate that you have them. Frequent travel and fresh horizons keep you feeling mentally and physically fit, so as you get older you should be able to maintain your vitality and youthful looks; your mental energies will never leave you. You want to be truly alive while yet you breathe, so there is a good chance you will make a very colourful splash on the canvas of your life. You will probably continue to acquire knowledge and assimilate information from the newest and latest of what's available even in old age.

The obvious careers for you to grow into are travel, sales, or anything involving dealing with the public. Film work might appeal because of its variety, as will writing and advertising. As the 5 is your Birth Force, don't worry if these are not your first choices; you might well spend time doing other things on the way. No-one is more likely to enjoy changes and new directions – indeed, completely fresh paths – than you.

The negative aspect of number 5 that you must watch out for is an overall tendency to lack real application and perfect the many talents you have: 'Jack of all trades, master of none', possibly. Sometimes, too, your over-analytical, clever mind can appear unsympathetic towards others. But most people come to realise that, without you, the world would be rather humdrum, so you are welcome at parties, functions and in offices.

YOUR 5 LOVER

This is the best thing that ever happened to your sex life. Your charismatic, funny, bouncy 5 is the most arresting person on the dance floor, full of original moves and wearing dazzling clothes. Everyone understands what drew you to him or her: when your 5 laughs, or talks, or flashes that charming smile, no-one else is even in the room. The only thing you have to worry about is how to keep other people's hands off your lover.

A 5 in love is a sight to see: if you have captured your 5's heart you will be wooed with energy and variety. Hopefully, you love to dine from the cuisines of different countries almost nightly: if a restaurant is out of the question, watch while your 5 flicks his or her wrist over the wok or the couscous pot to provide you with mouthwatering journeys for the stomach and the soul. Equally, you may have a picnic hamper packed for you to enjoy on a cliff's edge or a friend's yacht. A 5 lover never seems to run dry of inspiration for courting you in myriad ways and places.

Your lover's taste is progressive. His or her home is decorated with modern colours and functional but aesthetic modern furniture. Or, if they run to a taste for antiques (which is rare, but not unheard of) your 5 can blend the old with the new in a way that amazes others. You will also find the kitchen well-appointed, the bathroom full of sensual treats (massage oils, zingy shower gels, even the elixir of youth, perhaps) and the bedroom a suitable stage set for your erotic delight. A 5 lover will exhort you to all kinds of acrobatics and help you sexually to unwind completely. This is a serious lovemaking partner and you will be impressed, again, by his or her variety, technique and, perhaps best of all, humour carried into the bedroom... simply divine!

5s like to dress in interesting styles and colours to match their bright sparkly personalities, but somehow their choices are always in good taste as well. You can comfortably buy him or her designer clothes, as long as they show real flair and originality: your 5 hates to be like anyone else. If the wardrobes are full when it comes to present-giving time, simply buy a tennis racquet or new pair of trainers: this is someone who is good at all sports.

And the bad news? Well, yes, I'm afraid there is some. This is a naturally popular and sexy person: admirers will come more in packs than in pairs. Also, loving variety as he or she does, 5s can be guilty of short-lasting relationships. If you are going to beat the high turnover, you'll need to have plenty of different roles to play yourself as lover and an ability to countenance the inevitable flirting without falling apart. But if you love travel, laughter, sex and even danger, this is the one for you.

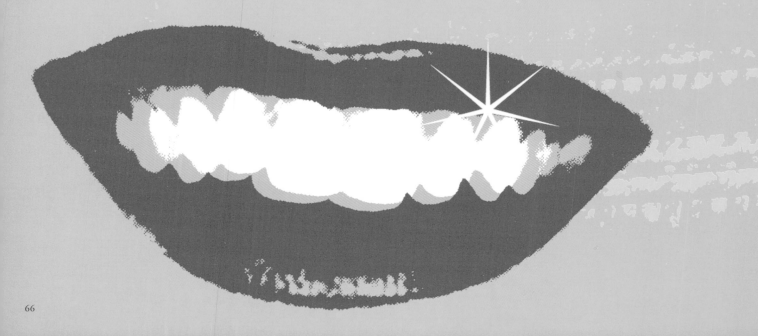

The 5 Child

Here's a young person designed to keep parents on their toes. No use being informed about yesterday's science and technology, or who was number 1 in the pop charts last month; your talented offspring will always be up-to-date with progressive ideas and information. You will have to work hard to gain street cred with this child.

In youth a 5 excels at sport and drama, in fact anything which requires energy and enthusiasm. They will be very popular with their friends at school and even the teachers will be impressed by their charm and intelligence. Enrol them for language and dance classes (yes, even the boys) and put their names down early for student exchanges abroad. Your 5 babe will love you for understanding their need for freedom.

Oh, and let them take a turn in the kitchen: though naturally not as good at cooking as 6s and (to some extent) 7s, they love unusual food and like to practise international cuisine. So, if you don't mind getting every pan in the house dirty, buy them an apron and some exotic cookbooks and stand back. You'll be as impressed by their entrepreneurial chit-chat about the ingredients as by the food itself. In short, this is the perfect progeny for parents who like to live life in the fast lane. As Hamlet said: "Let be!"

THE 5 BOSS

Chances are that this is the boss who is never at his or her desk. Travelling perpetually as part of their work, or at least always on the move from site to site, floor to floor, you'll have a job to keep up with your 5 boss's expectations. In a sense you'll have much freedom, always deputising for him or her and keeping everything else ticking along through your own initiative. And, on the good side, your 5 boss is quite generous, very funny and appreciative of what you do (which may sometimes involve covering for him or her). Always be well-dressed for this stylish individual.

THE 5 EMPLOYEE

This is a helpful and cheery soul to have around. Apart from occasional collapses from nervous exhaustion and the intensity of passion in their private life, a 5 working for you will make the whole business environment dance along with laughter, energy and good will. A 5 works well if given specific instructions, then left to get on with finding the best way to achieve that end; but be warned: it may not have been your way. But a 5 will find a dynamic way of getting results and charging the atmosphere with positivity and determination as well.

THE 5 HOUSE

You will hardly ever stop at home here for long. A 5 house is going to be travelled away from, or even rented out, or possibly change owners very often. If you want a place as an investment: perfect. It may be a gamble, requiring money, energy and time spent on it to bring it into the peak of its potential. But if you want a cosy family house, this may not be the best choice. Of course, as an address for a couple in the first flush of passion, it's ideal.

THE 5 LETTERS

E, N and W are the letters with a value of 5; a large number of any of these letters in your name, or a first-name initial of one of them, will give you some of the nervy, energetic characteristics of this number. If you are a 5, you need one of these letters in the name you use to bring out the full potential and strengths of the number. E will give you a very pithy humour, N a good imagination, while W will provide extra qualities of personal magnetism. If you are a 5 who lacks one of these letters altogether, you may experience regular attacks of nerves.

THE 5 PET

You know if your four-legged friend is a 5 because they can't sit or stand still. This is the dog that impatiently brings the lead in its mouth, the cat that jumps up suddenly and wants a change of scene, the horse that doesn't understand 'walk'. If you're looking for a companion to keep you busy and physically fit, this is the best pet. Not for them a curl-up by the fire (well, anyway, not for long). Give them a varied diet, as well.

WHAT HAPPENS IN A 5 YEAR?

To calculate the year cycle you are in, add the numbers of your birthday and month to those of the current year (rather than the year of your birth) and keep adding until you arrive at a single digit. This twelve-month cycle runs from the date of your birthday within that year until the eve of your birthday the year following.

A temporary cycle under the number 5 is a moment for extraordinary events, physical energy and impetus to get on with things; also in all probability passion, travel, a break into more freedom and some form of change to your lifestyle.

A 5 year cycle will see an intensity in your expressions of moods and feelings: you are suddenly subject to the stirring of romance; joy and contentment are the promise of this cycle. Happiness emanates from you for all around to see; you will feel beautiful and self-accepting. Everything around you may take on a new kind of beauty and energy: you may become acutely aware of the magnetic appeal of people and things you might not have noticed before. This whole vibration is connected with pleasure, abundance... and fertility.

This could be called a lucky time in your life, but in truth the joys you experience now are a magical, universal 'thank you' for all that you have done for others in the past. In career and business terms you should now be rewarded for your past efforts; you will also discover a newfound confidence in your abilities and judgements, which will enable you to go from strength to strength. Your associates and friends will be full of compliments, but they will mean everything they say. You do look wonderful and even, somehow, younger. You are sparkling and positive, inspirational to others and a pleasure to spend time with. You are sexy and mischievous, but everyone is charmed.

There are creative powers inspiring and directing you. You will feel encouraged to put time into artistic endeavours quite beyond anything you have done before; this may possibly be a result of your response to the beauty inherent in all you see and feel. Effectively, you are changing: your experiences seem more vivid, your observations and physicality more intense. Apart from the surge of talent you experience you could now feel a little romantic magic. If you have been alone for some time, this number cycle could be the moment for you to discover and meet the love of your life. Sometimes under this vibration a love from the past reappears, perhaps quite out of the blue. As with all 5 year cycles you are experiencing considerable change, and this change in you is evident to those close to you. The love from the past has probably changed too and circumstances may now be less prohibitive and more amenable.

The romantic note of this period touches existing relationships too. This may be the time when you and your partner decide to strengthen your tie and a proposal may suddenly seem appropriate. Your love might take on a deeper meaning, but you will nevertheless experience a sensation of lightness and good humour in each aspect of your life with the one you love. You may both have learned the true meaning of unselfish love. During this time of gaiety and passion you will have an increased chance of fertility, so news of a pregnancy is possible. This could be wonderful news, but if you're not sure, take care.

This numerical cycle brings love, but there is also good news ahead for you in your business life. New opportunities and better conditions will be on offer, but you must take your time deciding which course to take, as it will affect you for years: hasty actions or impulsiveness in your work affairs could lead to some losses. The days under this cycle are like the balmy, lazy, loving days on the best summer vacation, so relax and enjoy them. It is a creative moment, potentially very fulfilling, and if you act calmly and wisely you can look forward to realising some of your wildest dreams.

SIX

THIS CHAPTER REVEALS THE NUMBER OF BEAUTEOUS CALM AND LOVING, GENTLE FEELING. SIX IS THE NUMBER OF IDEALISM, SYMPATHY, UNSELFISHNESS AND HARMONY. NO NUMBER HAS MORE INSTANTLY RECOGNISABLE TRAITS THAN THIS ONE: MEET A SWEET, SENSITIVE SOUL, OF EITHER SEX, WHO IS INSPIRED BY THE ARTS AND MUSIC, WHO COOKS WELL, WHO IS A GREAT HOST, AND NEARLY ALWAYS VERY GOOD LOOKING, AND YOU'RE ALMOST CERTAINLY TALKING TO A 6.

NUMBER 6 WORKS FROM THE HEART: THE SOUL OF A 6 IS CONSTANTLY OVERFLOWING WITH FEELING. HE OR SHE WILL JUDGE WITH THE HEART, AND JUDGE FAIRLY; AND 6 STRIVES TO BE BOTH BEAUTIFUL AND USEFUL, PRACTICAL AND A DREAMER. ALL OF A 6'S SENSES ARE HIGHLY CHARGED. YOU ARE DEALING HERE WITH A VERY SENSITIVE SOUL, AND THEIR NUMBER IS THE NUMBER OF LOVE. THUS, ALWAYS ACT LOVINGLY TOWARD A 6 AND NEVER DESTROY A 6'S SOARING SPIRIT. IN EXCHANGE, YOUR 6 WILL BEAUTIFY YOUR SURROUNDINGS, BRING PEACE AND AFFECTION TO YOUR LIFE AND BE THE KINDEST SOUL ON EARTH.

THE LETTERS OF THIS NUMBER ARE F, O AND X. THE COLOURS ARE ROSE PINK, PALEST PINK, SCARLET AND HELIOTROPE. THE SCENTS ARE MINT, PINE AND PEPPER (FOR OVER-ATTACHMENT AND EMOTIONAL CLARITY) AND LAVENDER AND GERANIUM (FOR LOVING EMBRACE). A 6 FUTURE YEAR CYCLE ALWAYS FOCUSES ON LOVE AND DOMESTIC ISSUES. THE ASTROLOGICAL EQUIVALENT IS LIBRA.

Day Force 6

The Day Force number is derived from the day of whichever month you were born, so you are a 6 if your birthday falls on the 6th, 15th or 24th of any month. The number influences you in the most obvious ways, every single day of your life: friends will usually recognise you best by the characteristics of your Day Force number.

All 6 Birthdays

A Day Force of 6 is a gift from the gods. You have a beautiful outlook on life and hope to find the best in everyone. You are wise and have a strong sense of your own moral principles, and you need a peaceful environment to nurture your regard for other human beings. Your sense of service is very strong – sometimes in truth to the point of self-sacrifice – and you expect honest dealing from other people in return.

As a 6, harmony is a key word for you. Your aesthetic sense is very highly developed, so you want your decorative surroundings to be beautifully balanced. This often means that your taste is more conservative than cutting-edge, but you have a feeling for how to place all objects, colours and styles together so that they harmonise and make others feel uplifted and happy.

This will be especially true at your dinner table, which offers a treat as much to the visual senses as to the palate. Food is something you do really well (many of the best male cooks are 6s); you seem to get everything just right by instinct. You want your guests to feel at home with you, so there is no holding back on either food or wine.

Not only is 6 the number of love, but also of music. A 6 will often have a beautiful, musical speaking voice as well as a fine singing voice, and loves music in the home, the office, the car. Music is another vital dimension of mood setting; if you're a 6 you know how to employ it well. You probably play an instrument yourself, but if not, you know which are the right sounds with which to envelop your senses whether you are invigorated and jubilant, or tired and emotionally stressed. Music is a cocoon in which to wrap yourself; it will heighten your highs and ameliorate your lows.

Despite your aesthetic streak and gentle personality you are physically very strong and can work for hours at any kind of toil. Once you are engaged in something you will wish to see it through in one bout. This tireless energy in a worthwhile cause often lends itself to teaching young children, or to physically demanding artistic work such as interior decoration and painting.

And now we come to love: as vital to you as the air you breathe. To love deeply, and to be loved, is a major concern for a 6. You are influenced by every emotional act in subtle ways from childhood and the happiest 6 has enjoyed a secure and peaceful home in early life. A broken heart will leave a 6 traumatised for years, and despite extraordinary talents in the arts and in service towards people, a damaged or unfulfilled love life will prevent a 6 from achieving the satisfaction and expression of his or her true soul. But, if you are a 6, guard against a difficult tendency to idealise others, to build them up beyond reality and thus be destined for inevitable pain and disillusionment. You must try not to swamp others with your love: it may take you some years to find this out.

BIRTHDAY ON 6TH

People born on the 6th of any month have a deep love of nature, home, family and friends. In fact with this birthday there is a very deep vein of humanitarianism in you. You want and need to be loved and to love, you will seek out and thrive on approval from family, loved ones and co-workers, and will be miserable if you feel neglected or unappreciated.

This pure 6 birthdate usually implies that its holder will be an especially good cook – male or female – who will probably never need to follow a recipe very closely. You are imaginative, intuitive, creative and love to beautify all you touch, creating a magical environment which blends visual harmony easily with comfort. You will get on incredibly well with children, becoming one of them as required.

This birthday can be stubborn and argumentative, but usually your sweet-temperedness will be restored after a moment's reflection. 6s are also very gifted musically, even though sometimes untrained, often with a beautiful singing or speaking voice. You probably automatically see things in visual terms and will decorate and embellish with very good taste.

6s sometimes have an interest in group affairs, in helping neighbours and friends through difficult patches; you are probably a very good listener. Workwise you would succeed in any field which engages your artistic eye, sense of fashion and beauty and ability to make people feel cared about. You will possibly have a real interest in health and diet, and might work happily in this area. Music, interiors, graphics, fashion (especially accessories), art, food, or any business working closely with and for women are your forte. Born on the 6th, you will probably also be quite lucky with money.

BIRTHDAY ON 15TH

Those born on the 15th are loving, warm people – with this Day Force you will be a good friend and helpful associate to those close to you. You will be capable and independent, yet will make time to help other people: you will actually gain a sense of genuine accomplishment from sorting out the dilemmas of others and people will rightly see you as sympathetic and feeling. You are also very forgiving of other people's mistakes and understand when sometimes things don't work out quite the way you would wish.

Like those born on the 6th, if you have this birthday you will probably be an inspired and inventive cook, but this may not be your ambition. Your home will probably be important to you and you will be most content if you have a settled domestic background. You must also be allowed to give full force to your loving, romantic nature. You will make an excellent parent or teacher (even, perhaps, to your own parents), and you will have the good fortune to attract sincere friends, unexpected gifts and sudden opportunities.

You are a keen observer of human nature, who will use this faculty to absorb facts and gather knowledge: your understanding of life may well come from perception rather than study and research. You seem to have an inexhaustible youth and vitality, making you a sparkling companion. You are undoubtedly artistic and creative, with a good ear for music and probably a good singing and speaking voice. In business, any intellectual or artistic outlet will suit you, particularly fashion, interior design, publishing, medicine, food, music, singing, costume design or the beauty business.

BIRTHDAY ON 24TH

This birthday is usually connected with longevity. You have an excellent chance of making a financial success of your life provided you can actualise your ideas and don't just dream about what you might do.

Your family are going to be very important to you, both as a child and as a caring and inventive parent yourself. You will enjoy your home and want to make it look and feel inviting and welcoming. You, too, are an excellent cook, not needing to rely on recipe books. You are good at communicating with very old or very young people, which sometimes infers that you will have the responsibility of caring for elderly members of your family.

Your negative tendencies are towards jealousy and worry; you cannot help finding fault in others and you can also be terribly stubborn. If, however, you make use of your energies by remaining active, there is no limit to what you might accomplish, as you are very talented in almost all the creative areas of life.

You could be gifted in fashion, all areas of design, music, art, and writing. You might choose to act or simply to be in a position to do a lot of talking to others. This birthday bestows an ability to make speeches and address a gathering, which you do with charm and without pretension. You may be the natural MC in social situations, the person to whom others look for a few well-chosen words to say at the appropriate time.

Careers that come with this birthday reiterate all the fields of creativity described above, as well as banking, teaching, the restaurant trade, medicine, healing, therapy or beauty work. Money will come to you easily if you can focus yourself. With your ability to speak well, bear in mind that you would be better off pursuing your goals in person or by phone rather than by letter: you can usually talk someone round with genuine charm and grace.

Like all 6s you need and want to be loved, perhaps longingly. Oddly enough, you may fight your impulse to love, or not really believe that anyone can meet the standard of emotion you feel is necessary for your happiness. You must try not to intellectualise, but learn to follow your feelings. Having said that, beware of investing too much in someone else's perfection: you must love a real person, not a fantasy.

BIRTH FORCE 6

Your Birth Force number is calculated by adding together all the numbers of your date of birth and reducing them to a single digit (unless you arrive at 33, a kind of Master Number version of 6, in which case see page 140). Unlike the Day Force, which is clearly operative daily, the Birth or Life Force asserts itself over a lifetime. You will become aware of its strengths and weaknesses through your life, and must discover how to make the best of this ultimate direction.

A Birth Force 6 suggests you will learn how to express your emotions and feel deeply, as well as how to utilise your creative talents and artistic spirit. You will gain an interest in religious or philosophical beliefs, and always be guided by a strong sense of duty. Your humanitarian instincts will gradually strengthen; you will learn to offset stubbornness with compliance, and to read the emotional needs of those you love – though at first you seem reticent to do so. You will make your home your castle.

If your life number is 6, this usually indicates that you will grow into responsibility over many years, even that your path may at times be to support the person closest to you. Yours is not always a role that places you centre stage; it may be your karma to act as adjunct to your life partner. This is typical of the selflessness often called for from a 6. It is especially true if the numbers of your birthday total 33, which is a kind of Master Number (see page 140). You are here to learn to give – and that giving may take any number of forms.

As a 6, you will gain wisdom as your life unfolds. Part of that wisdom is evident in a gentleness of manner and approach to other people: in this way you achieve your own needs not with force but by steady, kindhearted co-operation. Part of your character is to teach, to heal, to help others: this will manifest itself in some of the vocational paths you choose. It would not be uncommon for you ultimately to become a philosopher, teacher, minister, historian or writer. You may also discover a real talent for healing and become a doctor, therapist, social worker or osteopath; or you will learn to express deep urges to paint, decorate, or play music.

Your pleasures come from other people: like the 6 Day Forces, you may become a great cook, host or connoisseur of fine wine. You will generously share what you have, inviting friends to your table perhaps more than is wise financially. However, the gods are with you: 6s always seem to land on their feet financially. If you don't earn it yourself, then you will come `to it by luck or default: it may be that your partner will be the high earner, or that you are remembered by someone in their will.

In the end, success is less important to you than a peaceful and happy domestic and love life. Across the years you will learn what is really important to you and, once you have found someone with whom to share your life, there is an excellent chance that you will find the right approach to keep things gently humming along. You are less likely to burst into fits of rage or passion and more likely to understand the need for patience and diplomacy in a relationship. But you do need to love and to be loved. If a love relationship does become stale, and you meet someone who rekindles your true feelings of affection, there is a definite danger that you will follow your heightened feelings. And indeed, this may be best for your health and happiness in the long run. You cannot survive without affection and warmth.

Loyalty to a parent or an early letdown in love sometimes causes a 6 Birth Force not to marry at all. But in any case, true love will probably come late as a reward for kind service and help to others in your life. The world will learn to recognise, in time, that you are truly a wonderful person, with a good heart and many talents, yet without the need for great accolades or public admiration.

YOUR 6 LOVER

Unless you are an unusually demanding person, you should be able to be really happy with your 6 lover: a 6 in love is loyal and affectionate, wanting nothing so much as to make you happy and find peaceful co-existence in your sunshine light. This is so romantic and, indeed, 6s are amongst the most romantic of all numbers, so handle their sensitive souls with care.

Your 6 love spoils you, taking care of those hundred bothersome tasks and making sure the everyday necessities for a secure life are dealt with. Your 6 also knows from the soul how to cook and will probably assume dominion (but without arrogance) in the kitchen. All 6 love affairs should thus go with the warning that, if your beloved is a 6, watch your weight.

A 6 in love beautifies his or her environment: the bedroom will be decorated harmoniously, they will have a fine CD collection, a knowledge of art and a taste for the theatre. After an evening performance they will know just the right restaurant to go to so that the inspired, romantic mood carries on; and they will place themselves unreservedly in your hands for adventures in mood, food and love. Though not as raunchy as 5s, 6s have finesse: they chalk up what you like and they don't forget.

This lover has soul, can be moved to tears and will trust you to the point of self-damage. He or she really responds to your efforts to beautify and harmonise your world for them. True, they can be guilty of overstepping the mark, doing too much for you, even smothering you with heavy affection. If you feel overpowered, gently express your needs so that they do not feel rejected, lost or threatened; this should produce a satisfactory result. Try to remember that many of a 6's failings come from a truly protective urge.

A 6's friends will seek them out for advice, warmth, reassurance and counselling about their own love affairs: this is not a threat. 6s are generally very loyal unless they are not getting the love they need at home. Their home life is crucial to their happiness: finding security and fulfilment there is a priority.

Love is important to a 6 suitor, who will choose ways of wooing you very carefully. He or she will dress with consideration, displaying flair yet good taste, making sure the colours balance and the styles suit. He or she is usually very good-looking and dresses comfortably. 6 is not a slave to fashion, but is always well turned out, often choosing tactile or flowing fabric to express an artistic but slightly old-fashioned preference for what is classically lovely. You can also be sure that your 6 love will certainly notice and appreciate it when you look fabulous.

And the negative traits? He or she can become really obstinate, or even possibly too compliant, so that you wonder where their strength lies. And, similarly, 6s can become doormats if their partners or family abuse their good nature. So this is partly up to you: talk your 6 humorously out of feeling sorry for him or herself and, if you feel you need it, do demand a little fresh air sometimes, so that you don't feel too strangled. As the old saying goes: 'How can I miss you if you never go away?' But all in all, this is a small price to pay for a truly loving, caring, kind human being – a lucky find indeed.

THE 6 CHILD

It is important that you nurture a 6 with great feeling and sensitivity from the cradle. Whenever you argue, you tear at the soul of your 6, who needs familial security above all things. This is the child to cuddle, to treat gently; this child is the most generous (along with 8s), the sweetest, the most honest and willing to please. Encourage their natural ear for music, listen to them give concerts, understand their very grown-up-sounding problems, take in their stray pets and wounded friends.

Your 6 child is intelligent and artistic, and loves to decorate their own space. Let them create a haven for their peace and security of mind: you will probably find they are naturally neat, in clothing and environment, and quite hardworking. True, laziness can be a problem, but usually only if your 6 isn't motivated. On the other hand, they will respond well to your trust, so let them cook (they'll become truly excellent at this), entertain your guests, do domestic chores for you. Your 6 understands your burdens and responsibilities, and is more flexible about this than many numbers. They also know when you need a cuddle, and are willing to provide one. Your 6 child is a great counsellor, a loyal friend and a gentle being. Let him or her grow up with plenty of love and aesthetic grace to bring out their most positive and alluring qualities. You should be a proud parent.

THE 6 BOSS

Really quite a pussycat – even when he or she means to get tough, it's not the real thing. This is a reasonable human being who will appreciate your loyalty and honest work; who will ask nothing more from you than he or she is prepared to give as well. To boot, you will probably get to work in a cheerfully decorated space with excellent office lunches regularly on offer. But don't be fooled: your 6 boss is dutiful and wants the job done, however sweet they are. Give lots and you'll get plenty back.

THE 6 EMPLOYEE

The whole office and everyone with whom they come into contact is charmed witless by this sweet-voiced soul who is always well-dressed, has excellent manners, and also brings yummy lunches to work, willingly sharing bites with all. A 6 works hard and well, is wonderfully honest and loves to create a peaceful environment for everyone. This is someone who brings flowers and never forgets a colleague's birthday. They may be a little old-fashioned, but this could be just what you prefer.

THE 6 HOUSE

The best for love! Always a house that will be beautifully decorated, this is a home in which to find marital security, peace for your children, as well as a haven from the mad rush of the outside world. Undoubtedly its past and present owners have endowed it with a wonderful kitchen. It should also prove a good investment – if you can ever bear to part with it.

THE 6 LETTERS

A preponderance of the letters F, O or X in your name will bestow affectionate, loving and artistic traits similar to the number 6 itself. If your first name begins with one of these letters you will both crave to be loved and be very loving yourself. These letters bring charm and good manners socially and also a wish to make a beautiful home and be proud of it. A lack of any one of these letters often brings deep emotional anxiety and reticence; too many of any one (more than three) creates extreme emotional cosseting.

THE 6 PET

This animal just wants to be patted, adored and soothed. Even if your 6 is a horse, it may be looking for a rug by the fire! A 6 pet is loving, gentle, loyal, home-loving and brings an angelic spirit into the family. They love food, so you'll have to watch their waistline.

WHAT HAPPENS IN A 6 YEAR?

A temporary cycle spent under any given number is worked out by adding the numbers of your birthday and month to those of the year you are currently in, rather than the year of your birth, then reducing these numbers to a single digit. If this produces a 6, you are entering a year where the primary concern is love, emotional security and happiness.

After a 5 'anything goes' year before this, you are now entering a more settled period when thoughts of romance or marriage and a renewed interest in the arts predominate. A temporary cycle of 6 is a fortunate one indeed, bringing a general feeling of warmth and well-being. You are relaxing after your 5 cycle last year and you are happy with yourself and others. Your home life also becomes very important.

During this twelve-month cycle you may be more than usually concerned with your appearance, and chances are that you will feel sexy, beautiful and bewitching. All 6 cycles deal with beauty and this one brings an extra radiance, so you feel much more self-confident and optimistic.

All your undertakings can prosper during this period. People in positions of influence help you financially and you will meet many who are utterly charmed by you. All of your stock rises: you do well with money, with friends, in your home, in your heart. Powerful associates or acquaintances will have regular contact with you throughout the year and much of your success seems to hinge on them. You will find that you are really in tune with the way others are thinking. Yet you do all you need in the gentlest, most unhurried way; there is nothing of the restlessness and pushiness you experienced in the previous cycle.

Number 6 always concerns love. This suggests a very strong bond with another person; you will have the urge to harmonise and be easy with someone you meet. And just as you are bound to feel loving, you may be as sure of your charms and appearance as you are ever likely to feel. It is probably your deeper qualities that will attract another under this cycle, but all the exterior trappings of beauty and fashion will boost your own sense of self. Marriage is governed by this number, so it may become a topic of discussion. Your family will also be relevant to you now, and their happiness will be brighter under this sunny spell of yours.

Your home takes on a new importance in the centre of your life at this time. It may not have been so important to you before, but now you will feel the benefit of having an environment in which you are happy. For this reason, a house change or redecoration project is very likely. The change of domestic arrangements might come from the strong love thread that runs through the cycle. You will be very lucky now and if you are shopping for a new house or flat you should find just what you want.

This period could be viewed as a harvest time: whatever seeds you have sown in the past, you now reap the fruit. Along these lines financial gain is imminent and your business dealings should prosper. You will have duties to discharge and you will need to be unselfish about your energies, but you will be repaid for services rendered.

The subject of art must surface in some respect during this cycle. You may feel compelled to take lessons, or if you are already skilled artistically you might decide to 'go public' with them. There is definitely a creative upsurge in your spirit and, whatever you attempt, you will find you do better than you could have imagined. Emotions are ruled by the number 6: if you can infuse your feelings into the activities you engage in – socially, creatively, in business or at home – you will discover a measure of satisfaction and talent that you might have been unaware of before.

The action this year unfolds relatively slowly, but surely. This is a year in which to catch your breath and enjoy yourself. And remember, you are able to understand and counsel the hearts and minds of others, which is required from you to fulfil your obligations as 6.

SEVEN

NUMBER OF MYSTERY AND PERFECTION, 7 HAS ALMOST APOCRYPHAL STATUS
IN NUMERICAL IDEOLOGY. THERE ARE THE SEVEN DAYS IN A WEEK, SEVEN
SEAS, SEVEN COLOURS IN THE RAINBOW, SEVEN LABOURS OF HERCULES,
SEVEN TRIBES OF ROME, SEVEN PILLARS OF WISDOM, AND OF COURSE,
THE MOST PROPHETIC SOUL BORN WILL BE, ACCORDING TO LEGEND,
THE SEVENTH CHILD OF A SEVENTH CHILD.

IF 7 IS ONE OF YOUR NUMBERS, OR IF YOU SHARE YOUR HOME WITH
A 7, YOU WILL HAVE HIGH STANDARDS TO LIVE BY. HEALTH, CLEANLINESS,
INTELLECTUAL ENDEAVOUR, DEEP THOUGHT, UNCONVENTIONAL IDEAS
ABOUT RELIGION AND PERHAPS A TENDENCY TO REFLECTION RATHER THAN
ACTION, ARE CHARACTERISTIC OF THE NUMBER. IN THIS CHAPTER YOU
WILL LEARN WHY 7S ARE OFTEN LONERS, SOMETIMES MISUNDERSTOOD,
DEMAND MUCH OF THEMSELVES AND THEIR LOVERS — AND ARE NEVER
INCLINED TO LEND THEIR TOOTHBRUSH!

IF EITHER YOUR DAY FORCE OR BIRTH FORCE NUMBER IS 7, YOU
NEED G, P, OR Y IN THE NAME YOU USE TO GET ALL THE STRENGTH,
ANALYSIS, INDEPENDENCE AND INTELLIGENCE FROM YOUR NUMBER.
YOUR COLOUR, AS A 7, IS BRICK-RED; YOUR SCENTS ARE GERANIUM, BAY,
FRANKINCENSE AND SANDALWOOD; THE ASTROLOGICAL CORRESPONDENCE
IS WITH VIRGO.

Day Force 7

Your Day Force will be 7 if the day of the month in which you were born was the 7th, 16th or 25th: the month and year are not relevant. This is the number which influences you most obviously from day to day, the part of your personality most seen by friends, and it governs the way in which you are likely to react spontaneously to all events.

All 7 Birthdays

In my view, this Day Force is the most complex, the most enigmatic, perhaps the most demanding, and probably the most interesting of all. You are your own best friend, and worst enemy. 7 is the number of perfection. This manifests itself as a burden of expectation on yourself and others, and intrinsically leads to disappointment and a possible sense of failure at the incredibly high standards 7s set for themselves. But it is certainly not all doom and gloom...

You are a shrewd thinker, considering things carefully rather than blurting out what's on your mind. This number brings great intellectual power and the ability to reason through anything. A 7 Day Force bestows a wonderful dry sense of humour and charm on its holder, which works in tandem with exceptional individual talents to assure an interesting, and potentially highly rewarding, business and personal life. You love your solitude and enjoy work which enables you to dig into problems and research information. You're not at your best working in a crowd and always prefer birds of a feather who understand both your humour and your independent way of doing things. Despite your charm of manner and personal dignity, you expect so much from yourself and from those who work and live around you that you need to develop a good relationship with those who are most important to you. It is not for you to chop and change like a 5, but to work at powerful, on-going bonds that will matter all your life.

On a lighter note you are almost certainly a wonderful cook – perfecting one or two preferred styles of cooking – really perfecting, whereas a 6 will dip into everything. You are just the same about wine, knowing not just a good wine, but its best vintage. You are not the dilettante: you are the professional. Half-knowledge will always frustrate you and you may take up courses of education at intervals throughout your life.

Like 6s, you love music, but you specialise. Intellectual 7s are serious, concentrated listeners inclined to collect, compare and prefer various recordings, artists or performances over years of experience. You are critical, because your powers of analysis work all the time. This does, more than occasionally, lead to some very funny but barbed remarks about films, theatre, concerts and so on. You always put your finger on a weakness – but beware, sarcasm can easily creep in.

Amusingly, you are known for having a great nose, so you sniff out and know at first whiff any perfume, food or wine from a distance. Many Day Force 7s utilise this talent in business; but it cannot be switched off, so a sweaty lover who is light on deodorant usage is not likely to last for long in your boudoir. And again, perhaps because of that nose, cleanliness is extremely important to you. You can be, at worst, seriously obsessive. Bath regimes and a spotless bathroom are requisite in the life of any Day (or for that matter, Birth) Force 7. If your life is as busy as it's likely to be, you'll have to get a regular cleaner in, or your poor partner will never be able to meet your demands.

The other crucial truth is that you need to work on your powers of self-expression emotionally. You don't give your thoughts away freely and those you love can be baffled by your true needs. This, coupled with your genuine wish for solitude, confuses your emotional life so that lovers may not realise you really want them in your heart. You seem to manage so well on your own, and you may think warm thoughts, but you seldom articulate them. Bear this in mind where relationships are concerned: bestow praise, thanks and affection whenever you can.

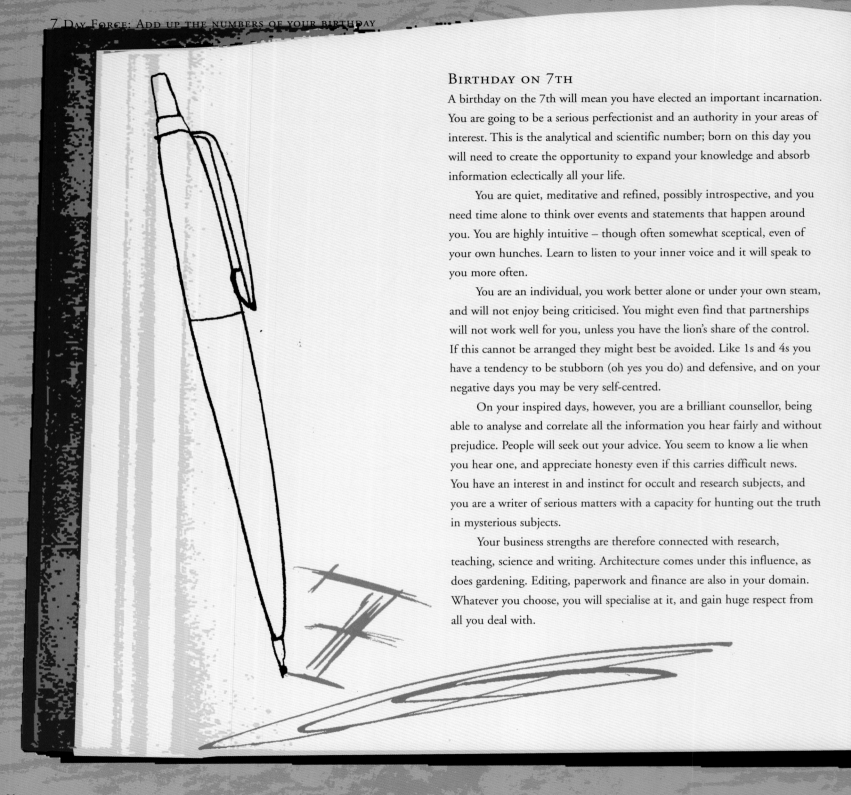

BIRTHDAY ON 7TH

A birthday on the 7th will mean you have elected an important incarnation. You are going to be a serious perfectionist and an authority in your areas of interest. This is the analytical and scientific number; born on this day you will need to create the opportunity to expand your knowledge and absorb information eclectically all your life.

You are quiet, meditative and refined, possibly introspective, and you need time alone to think over events and statements that happen around you. You are highly intuitive – though often somewhat sceptical, even of your own hunches. Learn to listen to your inner voice and it will speak to you more often.

You are an individual, you work better alone or under your own steam, and will not enjoy being criticised. You might even find that partnerships will not work well for you, unless you have the lion's share of the control. If this cannot be arranged they might best be avoided. Like 1s and 4s you have a tendency to be stubborn (oh yes you do) and defensive, and on your negative days you may be very self-centred.

On your inspired days, however, you are a brilliant counsellor, being able to analyse and correlate all the information you hear fairly and without prejudice. People will seek out your advice. You seem to know a lie when you hear one, and appreciate honesty even if this carries difficult news. You have an interest in and instinct for occult and research subjects, and you are a writer of serious matters with a capacity for hunting out the truth in mysterious subjects.

Your business strengths are therefore connected with research, teaching, science and writing. Architecture comes under this influence, as does gardening. Editing, paperwork and finance are also in your domain. Whatever you choose, you will specialise at it, and gain huge respect from all you deal with.

Birthday on 16th

Your birthday on the 16th labels you, too, a perfectionist. You are quite psychic and should learn to follow your hunches, despite a tendency to analyse everything over and over again. If you can listen to your gut instincts you will find that you are far more often right than wrong. You will find that your first impressions of people and situations will usually be uncannily accurate.

You must try not to brood over episodes in your past that have turned out less well than you would like: 16 is a number which often involves difficult experiences which demonstrate how to make the best of your mind and abilities (cold comfort, I'm afraid, but remember that you 'grow' through change). This could lead you to be over-critical of yourself, but you cannot change what has been. Begin each day afresh, and do not be your own worst enemy (this is worse for you, probably, than for any 7). You have a nervous disposition, can be moody and irritable, and may periodically withdraw into your own shell. You need your moments of stillness away from others, and you will find these especially rewarding in the countryside or by the sea.

You are not an aggressive person, but you can be quiet and aloof, resenting anyone's interference with your plans. The downside is that this could lead to a lonely existence, which would be a waste of the excellent analytical abilities you are capable of using to help others. When you are well tuned-in you will find you have extraordinary prophetic dreams or visions, and that you intuitively know the way things will work out for others. However, you may not be able to be quite so detached and accurate in your own affairs.

Pursue work in any field which allows you to specialise. Writing, teaching, law, analysis, detailed work, property and research would be some of the courses open to you.

Birthday on 25th

Your Day Force is the most intuitive of the 7s. You must learn to trust your hunches and encourage your inner voice to talk to you. You can be emotionally highly charged and moody, but you tend to conceal your real feelings, are reticent in expressing your needs, and can be misunderstood as a result.

You think long and hard before you speak, and may possibly be the best observer at any event – seeing everything but saying little. Excesses of emotion will affect your health and concentration, so you must learn to relax and stand back from your sorrows. You are a perfectionist in any area in which you bother to get involved; perhaps because of this you sometimes set too high a standard for yourself. This means you will be impossibly critical of yourself and those close to you. One of your faults is a lack of real faith in your ability. Do not underestimate yourself – if you just make a start you will constantly be surprised by your own achievements.

You will almost certainly be strongly inclined to music, with a natural gift for singing or playing an instrument. Learn to concentrate your efforts and try not to indulge yourself in melancholy, moodiness, laziness, and erratic behaviour. These are the negative trappings of your number if you do not lead a positive life. You can be truly happy leading a simple life in an idyllic location, needing no luxuries, but surrounded by books, a good music collection and being close to nature – especially water or woods.

You will succeed in any mentally demanding career where you can strive for perfection. In particular, the fields of art and architecture, computers, teaching, painting, woodwork or carving, writing, and research will be favoured areas of interest; or you might harness that nose, and work with wine, food or perfume!

BIRTH FORCE 7

To find your Birth Force number, add together all the numbers of your day, month and year of birth. Your Birth Force does not direct the way you respond to daily, spontaneous events; rather, over the course of your lifetime, the number 7 will come to describe your experiences, manner of dealing with situations and considered views on life.

When 7 is that number, you will find that over the years you learn to acquire great skills of analysis and deep thought. You will become an observant person who will prefer not to take things at face value, looking deeper for reasons and motivations. Your mind strengthens with the years, as will your patience and powers of concentration, so a combination of intuition and knowledge will enable you to succeed in independent business areas or paths of study, writing and research.

You will eventually recognise that you have a strongly reticent side to your nature which is an enigma to others, and you will prefer to select friends carefully rather than mix indifferently with a crowd. You are not a natural public speaker, either, but at home in your own areas of expertise you are a fount of riveting information and a very funny raconteur. You have a quiet magnetism which draws much respect and many close admirers, both in business and personal relationships.

You will often need solitude and really appreciate a monastic silence in which to think and recharge your batteries. Your number is connected with nature, water and the countryside, so you should find a growing appreciation for time spent in rural isolation (perhaps with just one other special, like-minded being). Reading and study will become increasingly important stimulation for your clever mind.

Don't be surprised when you react with anger if someone asks you personal questions: you prefer not to be asked about private matters outright and will guard your privacy jealously. You have no time for fools, so silly or intrusive questions and remarks are likely to elicit an ironic response from you. You will learn to keep your cool and much of your repartee will go over others' heads, because you enjoy being a little cryptic.

As time rolls on, you will gain an interest in cookery and possibly nutrition; 7 is a number concerned with health and hygiene, and you will enjoy simply cooked food perfectly done, handled with one clever stroke, as opposed to dishes overburdened with heavy sauces and creams. Your table is also likely to become increasingly minimalist in its presentation, as too your interior taste. You do not like clutter and appreciate well-made classical things. This should be true, too, of your personal style in fashion terms: clean lines, designer taste, plain shades without too much colour. You are admired for your elegant taste.

Business opportunities must eventually incorporate the talents of number 7, as your Birth Force increasingly asserts itself. You will enjoy working quite privately, and need no-one to push you along where your mind is engaged. You are skilled in educational matters, writing, law and history: a 7 loves to get to the truth at the bottom of things, so you may feel compelled to challenge traditional beliefs if they seem founded upon false premises. Your interest in health could also lead you to a career in medicine or alternative healing, and you may benefit from practising yoga and other forms of meditational/healthy exercise. You need music in your life, too, and will be a fish out of water if asked to do without it for long.

The negative traits you will have to wrestle with over the years are an unattractive tendency to be suspicious of everything (though you will sometimes have cause), to be unreasonable toward others, and to be too demanding of lovers and co-workers who have not your obsessive drive for perfection. You may also become over-analytical, never letting your mind rest, never accepting anything in good faith. Try to be less cerebral.

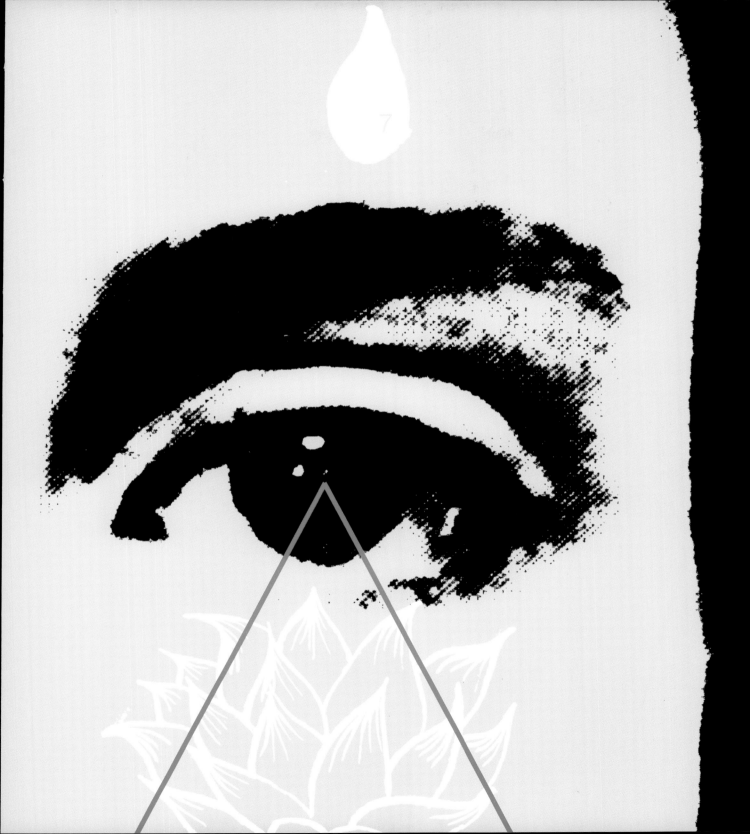

YOUR 7 LOVER

Perhaps you have fallen in love with a 7 because of the fascinating mind duel between you. You are naturally drawn to his or her lovely ironic humour and classy sense of style and taste; you may even like not knowing, from one day to the next, exactly where you stand in this relationship. A 7 is certainly a challenge.

To love a 7 is to love an intelligent and philosophical dreamer, someone who spends their time in their head solving the problems of a generation. Your 7 is not materialistic, but what they spend money on must be properly (perfectly) designed and made. Here, too, is someone with an impressive memory and breadth of reading, probably also musical, and with a proper learned understanding of art and the sciences. This lover can take you anywhere intellectually, sparking your own interest in subjects you knew nothing of before.

You also love your 7's critical judgement and refusal to play other people's games: there is something naturally aristocratic about a 7. He or she seems to be a bit of a loner, which again can be very attractive: will they make room for you on their desert island? This adds an element of mystery to the relationship. Of course this brings with it a downside: if you need emotional reassurance, you won't be satisfied here. You may never quite know how much you are loved, and this can lead to misunderstanding and stress. Equally, you will often feel shut out while your 7 delves inward in very private ways – and there is nothing you can do to prise this oyster-like soul from his or her shell. Best advice is never to take it personally – and it's really not personal, either. You've chosen a hard nut to crack, and you must acquire reserves of deep self-confidence in order to cope at times.

Your 7 woos you in a style like no other; his or her keen powers of observation will have quickly fathomed what you like, what will surprise and delight you. Restaurants by the water or in the forest (both 7 domains) will be favourite haunts, and you will be entertained by glittering, wide-ranging conversation. 7 knows too much: you'll never keep up, so just be graciously impressed. He or she will arrive for a date in pristine designer clothes (or the undetectable copies), clean and sunlight-smelling, ready to give you lots of personal attention. They prefer a one-to-one engagement to a celebrity party (even though they are quite likely the possessor of an invitation to such a glittering occasion).

You can make this relationship work if you give your love plenty of room to be alone at times, change your sheets more often than you ever thought necessary and always have a spare toothbrush! But be warned: you're on your own trying to understand what is bothering that over-analytical mind.

THE 7 CHILD

You may worry from the outset that this is a child who is too stressed about doing well in everything; but let them find their own way. From the moment of their first breath they are looking deeply at everything – never wasting words, but always asking for proof of anyone's assured facts. They will be cynical about every dictum and in some ways always slightly 'above' the company they keep. Yet this is a deeply emotional child who needs you to guess when a cuddle will be welcome, or when it will be an intrusion.

Your 7 child will practise music without being badgered, speak French with an excellent accent and, in short, decide to do well anything that they consider worth doing. He or she is critical of everyone: teachers, parents, friends. They will employ this critical faculty gainfully in their vocational life, but it can be very irritating to have to live with it. Listen carefully to what they say they would like to do: a 7 child will not skip wildly from one invented occupation or hobby to another, but will carefully consider what has the most resonance for them and then give it their all. So, whether it is painting, quantum physics or horticulture that has seized their imagination, support your offspring as best you can.

He or she may need some help with friends and relationships, because your 7 is sometimes misunderstood here. They appear so naturally self-sufficient that others are put off, believing themselves redundant or even actively disliked. 7s have not the words of light affection and hate making a fuss. They will be worn down by a humorous but persistent friend or admirer who is strong enough not to be put off by their emotional reserve. In short, your 7 progeny is a personification of the adage that 'still waters run deep'. But you will be consistently proud of their intelligence and self will.

The 7 Boss

A 7 boss works very hard, and expects the team to do the same. They are as self-critical as they are critical of anything you may do, but you need the confidence to know that the work you do is appreciated, for compliments are an unnecessary fuss for a 7. They expect no pat on the back, and usually forget to give you one; you must learn to read the unspoken remarks and understated smiles. On the good side, you will be working for someone with a refined and intelligent mind who is delighted to let you take time to perfect your work and who will work with you to achieve something of excellence; and, too, if you're invited for lunch, you'll always eat well. They'll keep you on your toes, and always be completely honest with you, and they won't insult you by looking over your shoulder all the time, any more than they would want this done to them. A trusting partnership.

The 7 Employee

Left to their own devices, this is someone who will constantly impress and delight you. Honour them with challenging work and they'll never need a kick in the tail to get it done. Charming and yet sincere, you can expect perfection always and an extraordinary degree of application to the specialist jobs. They are also always immaculately turned out, and speak to others expecting intelligent response. They neither appreciate – nor dole out – condescension. It is worth learning to accommodate their herbal slant on life and letting them practise yoga on the desk in times of stress!

The 7 House

A home for a connoisseur: here you can lavish your antiques and create a refined environment, with a good library and music room. But you may find you spend time alone, with loved ones away, for a 7 house is a place for meditation and quiet. Oh, and check all the plumbing and drainage before you buy: 7 houses are notoriously bad for water problems.

The 7 Letters

If you're a 7 you must use a name containing one of the letters G, P or Y, all of which have a value of 7 and boast some of its properties; this will help you to make the most of your mental strengths and powers of focus, as well as enhancing your diffident charm. If you have one of these letters leading your name, or many of them sprinkled throughout, you will acquire some of those same powers of critical thinking, plus an inability to suffer fools at all (never mind gladly) and the wish to think deeply before committing an answer. If you completely lack any one of these letters, you may be unsure of your mental powers, or never feel you have sufficient education, no matter how much of it you have acquired.

The 7 Pet

This is an arch animal – if you are trying to engage its attention for silly games you will be sorely disappointed in its refusal to join in, but possibly the subject of its wry amusement. This is an aristocratic beast, which may have deigned to choose you, rather than the other way about. On the good side, no pet will mind less if you want to relax, think and read; it can do likewise a few feet away from you. But don't cuddle the poor thing to death – this is a creature which craves its space.

WHAT HAPPENS IN A 7 YEAR?

Your future cycle number is worked out by adding the numbers of your own birth day and month (but not the year of your birth) to the complete number of the year that you are presently in. If, on addition, this comes to 7, then you will spend the twelve months from your birthday in this year to your birthday in the next year being governed by the laws of the number 7.

This is an important year, in some ways a sabbatical, demanding a rest from the battlefront, but always asking you to draw on tremendous personal reserves. You will find many demands placed upon your mental and organisational skills. Under a temporary cycle of 7 you may become personally very demanding of your own mental energies and wonder what you want from one day to the next. Quality and perfection are suddenly hugely important. The 7 years are often reflective and somewhat private, but this is not always the case. You may in fact now be quite restless, dying to do something ... but what?

When you feel you have settled on a line of attack, situations will arise that force you to rethink. People you would normally count upon and regard as reliable may let you down in little but nevertheless obtrusive ways. You will be tested at each turn of the path and find you have to check and double check your direction. These difficulties will be very draining and, though you can attain your goals under this cycle, no-one is going to hand you what you want on a silver platter. You will come through this by your own endeavour. The important thing to realise is that hard work and dogged persistence are the characteristics that will get you through.

Try to look at this year as a time for manifesting your goals by visualising them, seeing yourself triumph and continuing unfailingly toward the vision. If you lose sight of what you want, confusion rules. You may be tempted this way and that, distracted by gossip or calumny from others, and even attacked by those who love you but don't understand what you are doing. You cannot afford to be swayed, or you will lose your opportunities and lose precious time.

At the same time, keep your head. Do not react to provocation and try to avoid hasty actions and sudden decisions. A calm, gentle, unhurried approach is the best remedy for the chaos surrounding you. You may have to move house without much warning at this time, but take it in your stride and make a calm, clear choice when it comes to a new haven. Travel is also possible but must be undertaken with careful forethought and without pressure. If you are going somewhere exotic, be prepared with vitamins and medicines lest you suffer from indigenous bugs and diseases.

This is a cycle in which legalities often arise. They relate to business or, more probably, investments and house options. Consult an expert to circumvent potential oversights and, when you feel happy with the circumstances, proceed with confidence. If you have taken all the facts and details into account, you will now be within sight of your goal.

Watch your health, for the number 7 seems to be connected with this subject for good or ill. You may decide to get fit and lose some weight, or you may be besieged with many little health grievances. This is a time for mental, spiritual and physical house-cleaning, but also a time for rest: take a vacation in the country, to a quiet location where you can think in peace. Don't let others confuse you. You may have to watch and wait a little, but you will know how to survive if you listen to your intuition. This is also a great moment for study, research, writing and reading, and clearing out all the unnecessary junk in your life.

EIGHT

EIGHT IS A SPECIAL NUMBER: WRITTEN ON ITS SIDE IT BECOMES THE SYMBOL FOR INFINITY; THE NUMBER ITSELF REPRESENTS POWER. IT IS THE MOST MUSICAL (REPRESENTING THE OCTAVE), THE MOST STRONGLY CONNECTED WITH RELIGION AND ALSO REPRESENTS LAW AND JUDGEMENT, THROUGH ITS SYMBOLIC SHAPE SEEING BOTH SIDES OF THE STORY. IT EMBRACES AN UPPER WORLD OF SPIRIT AND PHILOSOPHY AND A LOWER WORLD OF PHYSICALITY AND MATERIALISM: BOTH EXIST FOR THE 8. SOMETIMES CALLED 'THE MONEY NUMBER', 8S SEEM TO BE FORCED TO EARN THEIR MONEY.

AN 8 IN YOUR LIFE WILL BE GENEROUS IN THE EXTREME, QUITE A BRILLIANT THINKER, WITH TREMENDOUS PERSONAL STRENGTH AND SOME IMPATIENCE TOWARDS SLOWER, LESS ORGANISED HUMAN BEINGS. AN 8'S HOUSE HAS THE BEST OF EVERYTHING: THEY WILL NOT WASTE MONEY ON RUBBISH, INSTINCTIVELY GETTING THE BEST OF WHAT THEY CAN AFFORD. A NEGATIVE 8 COULD BE TOO OSTENTATIOUS AND LOVE DISPLAY FOR ITS OWN SAKE — BUT MORE OFTEN, A BALANCED 8 QUIETLY AND AUTHORITATIVELY MAKES EFFICIENT USE OF TIME AND SPACE AND HAS A HEAD FOR COMPLEX MATTERS. AN 8 LOVES TO HAVE A FINE LIBRARY OF QUALITY HARDCOVER BOOKS.

THE LETTERS CORRESPONDING TO 8 ARE H, Q AND Z; THE COLOURS OF 8 (WHICH COULD BE WORN FOR LUCK WITH MONEY, FOR INSTANCE) ARE TAN, BRONZE, BUFF AND OPAL; THE SCENTS OF 8 ARE BENZOIN (RELIGIOUS THOUGHT), TUBEROSE (BALANCE), AND CEDARWOOD (STRENGTH, DIGNITY AND POWER). THE ASTROLOGICAL SIGN CORRESPONDING TO 8 IS SCORPIO.

DAY FORCE 8

Your Day Force is the number of your actual birthday, disregarding the month and the year in which you were born: you are an 8 if you were born on the 8th, 17th or 26th. The characteristics of this number will influence your personality and spontaneous reactions on a day-to-day basis.

ALL 8 BIRTHDAYS

As an 8, you are a high-minded and very powerful person. You understand that the infinite is possible and you have an awareness of that infinite – an inheritance of divine knowledge. You are drawn to, and at one with, the great mysteries of life: there is a kind of Hamletic element to your nature, a posing of the question 'To be or not to be' throughout your life. Every day you can see both sides to the problems that face you and others – like the two circles that make up the 8. You have both masculine and feminine qualities; you can be both passive and active, generous and penny-pinching. Your greatest personality strengths are realised when your talents are in balance. You must strive to comprehend, somehow, both heaven and hell – and you may indeed experience both, at least in a philosophical way.

You have an inherent gift for authority, so others will look to you for guidance. Your ability to see things fairly makes you an excellent arbiter and your intelligence finds a way through the most difficult situations. You can see without prejudice and you show wisdom in restraint. You are personally ambitious, yet your mind is not tainted with ill fellow-feeling and you cannot help achieving recognition. You expect a noble mind in those you deal with because of your own. You need to find a balance between your own wish to assume power and get things done and your instinctive moral integrity. This sometimes causes a tug, and most often results in a strongly humanitarian streak which attempts to satisfy both sides.

Money is a big issue for 8s; it is part of your destiny to experience all aspects of financial responsibility and power. You have more ability to earn – and earn well – than any other number; yet despite this, your rewards are not handed to you on a plate. An 8's fate is either to earn vast sums or to be beleaguered with money worries. Either option may dominate, but it is in your own power to direct this. It is your lot that you must (and will wish to) give your all, your very best efforts, to everything. 7s strive for perfection, but 8s know no moderation, adding this to a similar drive for excellence. You have, quite simply, the most outstanding abilities; you also know you have a requirement to use those abilities unselfishly. It is a load to carry, and you will be tested from time to time. You may make a fortune and lose it all in a day: but you will fight back. You may be forced to take financial responsibility for a partner or parent, and somehow you will win through with astonishing results.

You love music, perhaps more than any other number. Rhythm is in your tread. Number 8 rules the octave, so you require harmonious sounds that balance: discordant music is rarely to your taste. If your musical talent is not trained (a common problem for 8s, whose family life is not always conducive to the nurturing of their talents) you should make up for this in later life if you can. Making music will always bring you a release from strain and an expression of your quasi-religious soul. You also have a love of and talent for sport, perhaps because of that sense of rhythm and mental power. This is perhaps the only area in which you are physically active: in all else, it is your brain that is your power.

You are generous, loyal and honest in love, but can be guilty of two damaging faults. One is your tendency to self-recrimination through over self-analysis; the other is a neglect of your need for tenderness and love-making with your partner when the stress of work dominates (which will happen frequently). Ironically, when you love it is deep – a marriage of mind and soul – so you must ensure that you nurture the tie that means so much to you. This is especially so as love will soften the otherwise strong business and intellectual side of your nature.

BIRTHDAY ON 8TH

Born on the 8th, you have the money number operating as your Day Force in its purest form. You are progressive and creative, and will succeed in business if you can find the correct outlet for your talents. You possess executive ability, are a good judge of character and yearn to get on with something productive.

The 8th is considered the luckiest 8 birthday, but to make the best of it you must utilise every opportunity which comes your way or you may find you are in financial trouble. Avoid this by living a positive life and by learning to recognise your luck and be aware of your capacity to draw on what you need when you really need it.

You love to make an impression with people and can be very fond of 'peacockery'. You will probably want to own a large and impressive library, but may not read all you collect. The quality of what you own will be the very best of what you can afford. You possess a mind capable of great depth of thought and you may well be drawn to the occult side of life, as well as to a balanced understanding of many religious views.

Workwise, you need a broad field of activity in order to flourish; thus you would do well as a lawyer, an executive or company director, a high profile accountant, a buyer, in banking, in personnel, or as a member of an orchestra. Many musicians, especially composers, are born on the 8th.

8

Birthday on 17th

The 17th is also considered a fortunate birthday, though throughout your life you will be tested for your capacity to smile through stormy weather. You are high-minded and surprisingly conservative one moment, but extravagant and original the next. You are undoubtedly honest and straightforward in the main, but in business you can be calmly ruthless. Outside the work arena, though, you have a kind and considerate nature.

This number is not necessarily spiritually inclined, requiring proof of things beyond the physical senses. However, the number 8, which is your base number, is the karmic number (you get back what you give out) and as such rules the occult; so if you are thus inclined, you may have an inherent understanding of mystical and philosophical matters, and need no proof besides your own sense of probability.

Almost certainly you have a keen appreciation of music. You will care deeply about your family, be generous and proud of their abilities and achievements, and will be unlikely to forget birthdays of close friends or family. You can be swayed by your emotions, but are usually rather set in your ways. Once you have made up your mind you can seldom be moved from your chosen course.

You would succeed in any business if given a chance to use your executive qualities, and you will be happiest if you can delegate routine or mundane work. Some people with this birthday flourish in the world of banking and property; if you choose writing it should be in the area of non-fiction. An 8 must conjecture, must have a subject to contemplate, and this is most true of you with the numbers 1 and 7 both in your birthdate. All 8s have a profound interest in history and what has come before in the realm of thought. Thus you would be suited to work involving history or research, criticism (of the constructive kind), acting, theatre production, publishing, broking or taking the directive for others. Through its occult associations this birthday number also suggests an ability with astrology, numerology and psychic matters. It almost certainly means you will come to a position of responsibility, and if you concentrate and balance giving with receiving, you may amass a secure financial inheritance for your children.

Birthday on 26th

With this birthday you are fortunate in having a strong number for financial success and general good luck. You may have a taste for art, but you will probably do better in the field of pure business. You can be a wonderful organiser, even on a grand scale, and you need scope to allow yourself to develop this talent. Provided you do not sink into laziness or negativity you need never go without, for like all 8s your monetary fortune rests in your own hands.

You might start many projects and ventures but then leave them for someone else to finish, so you must try to concentrate your efforts. All 8s have a tendency to live a little in the past, even to fight progress – this may be especially true of you. Be optimistic and look to the future with enthusiasm.

You will love ceremony and the grand occasion, and would benefit from a good education both in books and in life – in the sense of travel and living abroad. You are a philosopher at heart, with a nobility of mind and purpose. Home and children will always be close to your heart. You can experience great cycles of moodiness, your feelings soaring and plummeting, but marriage or a stable relationship would help to balance this.

Careerwise you need a position of power and scope, with someone to whom you can delegate menial tasks. Law, publishing, education, accounting, music and corporate work, including conference organising and the like, may be your best areas of endeavour. You definitely need to work for yourself, or in partnership, being a boss rather than an employee.

BIRTH FORCE 8

As we have discussed, your Birth Force is 8 if the total numbers of your day, month and year of birth added together reduce to the single digit 8. However, should they total 44, you are a Master Number 44 (see page 141) but you might also find it interesting to read on, as there are similarities with 8.

If your Birth Force is 8, you have elected to learn all about power and distinction in the material world, but equally to learn that money alone will not buy a fulfilled life. Your challenge is to find the correct balance between achievement and philosophical enquiry.

As a child, an 8 Birth Force learns quickly to grow up; your life experiences bring you to a relatively early state of maturity regarding the human condition and the need for good organisation and mental discipline in order to make the most of our time on this planet. You have learned from many previous lifetimes, and from your early life now, how to touch the deepest secrets in other people, and how to plumb the depths of any given circumstances. This provides you with uncanny judgement and an instinct for fair dealing.

The two circles of the number eventually lead you to an understanding of the two sides to humanity: male/female, weak/strong, demanding/ yielding, joy/sorrow. You have these binary oppositions inherent in your nature and are the wisest soul in your overview of the serious circumstances of others' lives, always feeling equally both sides in any argument. Where others see only an entrenched position, your gift as an 8 is to see the possibility of balance.

You have the power to supervise and it is your energy that will get things done on behalf of a group. You have many burdens laid on you, but you get help from above to deal with all that is placed on your shoulders. It is vital that you look for this and embrace it. One of the difficulties of this Birth Force is that it takes many years for you to understand your great strengths – indeed, to understand yourself at all – for this is a deep number, and the mental power that comes with it takes time to grow into.

As soon as you realize that your exceptional business and intellectual talents – which include charismatic leadership of people – can lead to material gain, you will be on your way to the influence and recognition you deserve. En route, many trials will beset you, and businesses may chop and change until you find the best plane for self-expression. Repeated effort gets you there; you have been born with phenomenal strength, like a baby Hercules, but you must learn how to feel and flex those muscles. Once you see this, you will become a gentle, generous giant.

Mental strain is part of your diet. So, too, the frustrating periods when you have to prove yourself in adverse circumstances. But don't worry, you are equipped for this: be bold, dive into the deepest water knowing you can be self-reliant and will not drown. You will be asked to pick up the pieces of others' dreams and meld them, supervise them, into a cohesive whole. Where a 4 slogs through the small office, an 8's thinking is altogether broader – more akin to the corporation. You love to experience the thrill of a difficult project brought to realisation. Further, your impartiality to others helps you achieve harmony in the actualisation of your projects.

Over the years, you will come to be regarded as the Solomon in your family. Tough experiences teach you that there is more to life than just material success, and you can impart this vividly with the excellent visualising sense given you through the synthesis of 'male' rationale and 'female' feeling. You feel strongly about things and develop a noble spirit towards others. Your love relationships sometimes suffer while you're caught up with business pressures, but you will ultimately understand how to balance a busy life with all-important family strength. You are forced to take control of matters in your life again and again: there is no free ride for an 8.

YOUR 8 LOVER

Two schools of thought exist regarding an 8's love life: one is that an 8 will choose a partner for security rather than deep love, preferring a solid person with whom to have a family and secure home. But I don't subscribe to this theory, believing the other hypothesis – that an 8 is a deep thinker and someone who needs the balance of physical love with intellectual parity. In this sense, then, you will be best suited to an 8 lover if sex is not the only thing that draws you. He or she wants to delve deep into your soul and mind, wants to have intelligent discourse with you, and wants to believe in you as a cause worth fighting for to the ends of the earth.

Your 8 lover has had lots of sharp knocks in life – despite the appearance of success sitting easily on their shoulders. This lover feels strongly that there has to be more to a relationship than a quick tumble and light-hearted romance: life requires tenacity and relationships need stamina. The 8 can give you both – but if it sounds too serious for you, move on to a laughing 5 or an easy-going 6.

Assuming, however, that it is the depth and philosophical persuasion of your 8 that first drew you (as well as their amazing charisma and intelligent mind) you are more aware than anyone that this is a noble and generous soul. Your 8 emits an aura of class, style and, vitally, fair-mindedness. He or she will consider your ideas carefully, always looking for the best way to carry out your wishes and plans. You love your 8's dynamic personality, and you trust his or her demeanour of authority – which, indeed, others will willingly follow. You will also experience your 8 beloved as one of the most ethical and non-judgemental people you've ever met. All this is so.

This said, don't feel that your 8 will be a disappointment sexually: 8 has immense physical stamina and an understanding of the physical needs of life – through its astrological association with Scorpio this is also the number of sensuality – it's just that there has to be more to the relationship.

He or she dresses well, recognising that the world tends to judge a book by its cover; it is rare for an 8 to dress cheaply. If your 8 is one of the well-balanced holders of this number, he or she has a wonderfully playful sense of how to enjoy money and will shower you with presents. If they are a little insecure, they may wear too much jewellery or depend on designer items to give them credibility. But usually, your 8 has such innate power that there is no need to overplay the part.

Buy your 8 one quality gift instead of lots of little trinkets when it's birthday time: truly, one Lalique crystal glass will go down much better than half a dozen currently fashionable glasses from a lifestyle shop. Similarly, one beautifully designed, luxurious shirt will hit the spot far better than a whole outfit from the High Street. Your 8 likes quality far more than quantity – and this would be a metaphor, too, for their choice of lover.

Love your 8, cuddle him or her, and be playful when he or she gets bogged down in business. Your 8 worries about getting things just right all the time, and neglecting you sometimes is a mistake made through wanting to look after the bigger picture... be forgiving.

THE 8 CHILD

An 8 in childhood is still a wise old justice of the peace; family arguments are often effortlessly resolved with the calm and fair-minded intervention of the 7-year-old lawyer in the making. Don't try, ever, to get your 8 child to take sides in a dispute: it will cause them immense distress, because they can see both sides of every argument. This same sense of balance enables your 8 child to maintain disparately minded friends in one amazing cohesive whole, a crowd that would disintegrate if your child were not there to hold it together.

This is an intelligent human being, who needs intellectual stretching at an early age. Get him or her interested in philosophical thought and mystery stories that provoke deep consideration as early as you feel inclined. So, too, encourage their musical ability, for 8s are naturally rhythmical and are sadly often left without training of their musical gifts, which they will later regret. You may find your junior barrister is good at sport and games, too, so never begrudge them time spent on the playing field: it won't usually cost them a career in a more intellectual arena later. Or it may be that their astonishing self-discipline makes them an outstanding athlete in any case, which will later pay them handsomely. 8s never starve, being extraordinarily resourceful about finding ways to hold body and soul together.

Encourage that truly generous streak in your 8 progeny, for a gift unenthusiastically received ('You shouldn't waste your money on me...') will break something noble in their spirit. Of course, outright extravagance should be curbed, but always respond warmly to the generous nature in your child; ultimately, they will be able to afford it. Another important trait to promote is their interest in books: 8s love journeying in the mind and will delight in books that others might consider too serious. Best subjects: history, literature and finance; best character trait: strength of character, astonishing brain power, generosity of purse and professional time.

THE 8 BOSS

If you work for an 8, your business life is already in the fast lane anyhow: an 8 would only pick someone who showed intelligence and skill. An 8 boss should be a wonderful person to learn from: he or she has an excellent mind, incredible self-discipline and the power to put other issues to one side when work demands more than 'all'. Of course, this anticipates that you, too, will give one-hundred-and-ten percent to the job at hand, but your 8 is probably also a good patron at the office lunch, appreciates your intelligent contributions more than any other number and will share the profits with you in one sense or another.

THE 8 EMPLOYEE

This is someone waiting to go out on their own: all 8s rise to the top eventually, but understand they must learn everything they can to get there and will put in extraordinary effort as they progress on their own learning curve. One of the best strengths of your 8 employee will be their mental agility and toughness of character. After days of work on one project, if it has to be started all over again, your 8 is resigned and willing. This is someone who won't give up. But never be patronising to an 8 worker – they're going somewhere.

THE 8 HOUSE

A wonderful place for an investment, for you will surely make money with it. Even if you simply fell in love with its generous proportions, or seeming stateliness and offer of security and a comfortable (even luxurious) lifestyle, you will still find you cannot lose money on an 8 house. Even if it is only the size of a small cottage, the spirit of a manor house lurks in every 8 dwelling. It is also as solid as a rock and will rally you when life outside gets tough. An 8 home gives you a sense of authority.

THE 8 LETTERS

The so-called 'money letters' are H, Q and Z, which correspond to the properties of number 8, so if your first name starts with one of these, or if you have quite a few 8 letters in your name, you are absorbing some of the qualities of the number 8: business ability, power with money and mental acuity. H is a magnetic letter for drawing money and success; Q has an artistic streak and delves into the occult or other mysteries; Z is the most spiritual and philosophical, but has a fortune that snakes and ladders through life. If you are an 8 lacking any 8 letters, money may be a problem for you in life, or you may not be able to manage and hold on to what you earn.

THE 8 PET

This is the cat that likes to sit on the velvet throw rather than the mat, the dog that dozes for preference by the Georgian fireplace rather than the mere hearth. Your 8 animal friend likes the good life, but is an intelligent companion whose thoughts are always a step ahead of your own. Those dreams you see them having concern the problems of a pet's life – this is a deep-thinking beast. And, when you need to borrow a little strength to survive in a crisis, your 8 pet knows this and is there to lend a paw or hoof as required. A noble animal, indeed.

WHAT HAPPENS IN AN 8 YEAR?

The year cycle is calculated by adding the numbers of your birth day and month to the numbers of the current year (not your year of birth). It is a twelve-month cycle that stretches from your birthday to the following birthday.

All 8 cycles relate to karma, but none more so than 26/8: under this cycle you should receive pleasant repayment for all the nice things you've done in the past. If you have been the patient counsellor of other people's problems, now you will experience your blessings for it. Good news and loving messages abound; you will find that you look forward to the postman's arrival or the message light blinking on your answerphone. Nearly everything you experience under this vibration is joyous – unless you have been a real Ebenezer Scrooge in the past and denied friends your time and energy.

One of the more interesting associations of this cycle is the likelihood of connecting up with a soul-mate. If you are single, you could not have a better chance of meeting someone special than now. Oddly enough, because 8 years also relate to money, you may be snowed under with an impossible workload and regard the entrance of such a potentially strong love into your life as very poor timing. On the other hand, this may be why it comes now – it is often the case that a 'watched pot never boils', and your attention being given elsewhere may be the best reason for someone's ardent admiration at this time. In any case, the love vibration you experience now under the karmic cycle 26 is likely to point to your future marriage prospect (or, if you don't espouse marriage as the course you wish to take, at least you could regard this as your potential life-partner). Whoever comes into your life now will feature very strongly in your future life.

Pregnancy is governed by this number, in which case there should be a very special, reincarnated link between child and parents. Or, you may respond to a deep urge to study a subject which feels very familiar to you, though you have never learned about it before. A language that comes easily, an artistic skill you were attracted to and had never developed but which you now pick up, even a subject of professional interest that you seem to grasp as though you had studied it before (history, music, healing, etc), could suggest that you are returning to an area of interest which is carried through from another life. Your mind will be very receptive and you will extend your philosophies considerably.

If you use your good judgement under this influence, business and money matters should flourish. But sift carefully through the details of your potential investments and possible partners. No-one will think the worse of you for exercising caution, and the negative effects of this period (see above under Ebenezer Scrooge) would manifest as bad news, false lovers and deceptive partners. Contractual situations should be avoided and decisions may be hard to reach.

However, the positive side of this wonderful cycle promises the best for optimistic, strong-minded adults. Beautiful relationships, trustworthy business associates and happy social events take precedence, and you should soon be wondering why the year appeared to pass so fast.

NINE

THIS IS THE NUMBER THAT COMPLETES THE TRUE CYCLE OF 1 TO 9, AND REPRESENTS FULFILLED DESTINY AND PERFECTION. THE NUMBER 9 HAS SEEN ALL GO BEFORE AND, AS SUCH, IT ACQUIRES WISDOM AND AN ATTITUDE OF FORGIVENESS. IT IS THE 'MIRROR' NUMBER, REFLECTING ALL PEOPLE AND EXPERIENCES IN ITS OWN EYES. THEREFORE IT IS UNIVERSAL BROTHERHOOD, IDEALISM, BUT SOMETIMES A SENSE OF SADNESS AND MOODINESS, THAT SURROUNDS THE NUMBER.

A 9 IN THE HOME IS THE CLOWN AND THE ACTOR, PLAYING OUT ROLES, MIMICKING OTHERS. 9S ABSORB EVERYTHING THEY'RE EXPOSED TO, FOR GOOD OR ILL, AND, THOUGH THEY LIKE TO HOPE FOR THE BEST IN EVERYONE, THEY KNOW BETTER. THIS NUMBER, THOUGH, IS ENORMOUSLY FRIENDLY, ITS HOLDERS ARE WELL-READ AND SEEM TO THINK OF THE WHOLE WORLD AS THEIR OWN PATCH.

THE LETTERS BELONGING TO NUMBER 9 ARE ONLY I AND R (AS THERE ARE ONLY TWENTY-SIX LETTERS, THERE IS NO THIRD LETTER UNDER 9'S INFLUENCE); ITS COLOURS ARE OLIVE, STRAW, SMOKE, OLIVE GREEN AND MULBERRY RED; ITS SCENTS ARE HYACINTH (FOR MOODS), ROSE ATTAR (FORGIVENESS), ROSEMARY AND SANDALWOOD (FOR THE ROUNDED MIND). THE ZODIAC EQUIVALENT OF THIS NUMBER IS SAGITTARIUS, THE TRAVELLER AND ACADEMIC; AND 9 IN A FUTURE YEAR CYCLE BRINGS BOTH TRAVEL AND A HUGE CHANGE, AS IT COMPLETES THE FULL NINE-YEAR CYCLE.

Day Force 9

This is the number, remember, just of your actual birthday (disregarding the month and year of your birth) which influences your most obvious and automatic reactions from day to day.

All 9 Birthdays

As a 9, you are a reflective person whose daily responses are in fact tutored by the experience and wisdom gained over many lifetimes: it is of you that people say: 'You've been here before'. Any 9 birthday bestows a compassionate and easygoing nature on its holder. You get on with everyone, always finding at least one point of contact with any human being. As you will have travelled the world – either literally or metaphorically – you have seen enough of life to understand but not judge others.

To prepare you for a life of wisdom and benevolence toward others, 9s often experience many disappointments in life and are buffeted by the winds of change from childhood. Security is often the most elusive state of being for you; your earliest years may well have subjected you to family change and forced you to be adaptable. So must it be in adult life: circumstances may alter readily, but somehow you have it in you to cope with grace.

A 9 has a great bond with their father, which often asserts itself because their father has been absent or busy in their childhood, leaving them with a feeling of huge but unfulfilled longing about him. Or the father is indeed altogether missing and the child must search out a true image of him cerebrally. Sometimes this means a 9 has an active feeling of agony about their father: it is one or the other.

As 9 mirrors all the numbers – whatever number is added to 9, it reduces again to the original number (e.g. 5 + 9 = 14, and 4 + 1 = 5 again) – 9s are clairvoyant and highly intuitive. A 9 can see the need for separations and endings where other numbers will try to defy the inevitable. A 9 won't enjoy these losses, but they see how it must be, and cope.

Your excellent imagination and ability to empathise gives you exactly the right talents to act, paint and write full-time: theatre, in fact, would be a fruitful area of creative endeavour because all these talents can be used under one roof, as it were. The lust 9s feel for travel makes any business connected with it a good choice. If your actual business is not travel it will incorporate travel. To add to the list of talents, music comes naturally to a 9, as does any work requiring a degree of oratory.

Watch the negative trait of 9 to be a 'Jack-of-all-trades, master of none'; you are too talented, perhaps, and need to focus. Also, that changeable side of your character gets bored with one situation – in the workplace or in your personal life – so make sure you have freedom within the circumstances in which you live. It may also be important that you give up a lifetime's inclination to be liked by everyone. You haven't failed if you find some friends difficult.

In love relationships, your immense charm and realistic experience make you desirable and very popular; also, you seem to have done so much, and to have so many facets to your character. You need a very positive partner because of your tendency to absorb the mood of those close to you: a depressed partner will have you plummeting right alongside. The down side of a 9 in relationships is that you often can't help creating changes, so you may have many false starts before you find a lasting relationship.

You may be lucky with money, quite religious in your outlook (though not necessarily in a conventional way) and you will usually find the world at large very forgiving toward you when you do offend: you are so obviously not malicious, no-one can hold anything against you for long. Understand and enjoy your numerous gifts and awarenesses; and try to spend your coin of compassion wisely, without wearing yourself out.

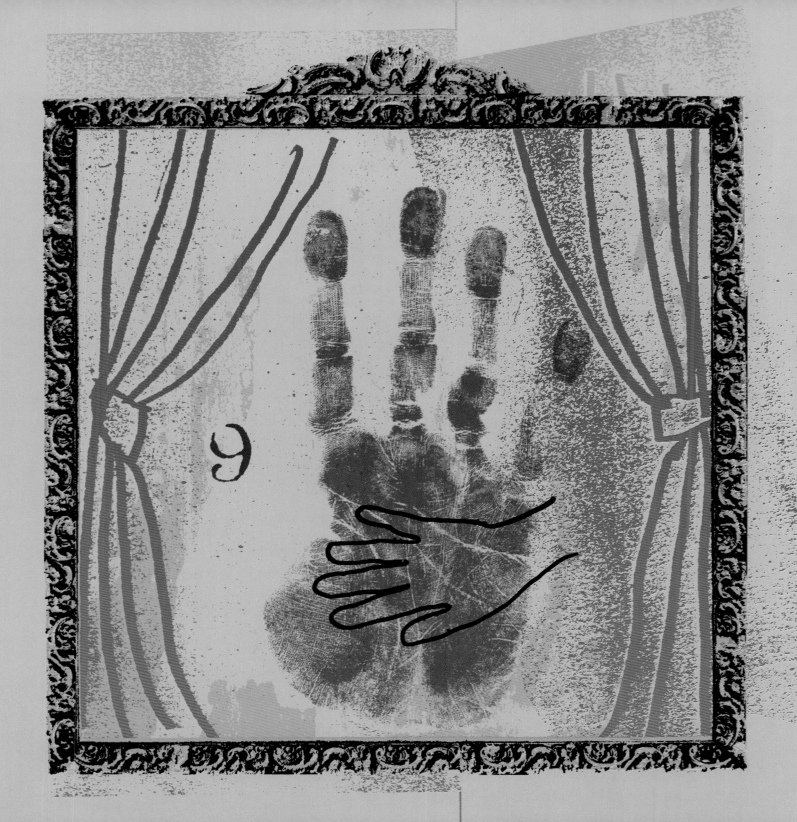

BIRTHDAY ON 9TH

The 9th is a wonderful birthday, embracing intellectual and artistic types who love variety and see things through to completion. You can be approached through your emotions and have a strong humanitarian streak. You are something of a philanthropist and must be given an opportunity to express your talents before the public. You may also be a gifted actor.

With a birthday on the 9th you will travel if you have a chance, and will experience many changes. You may suffer losses and separations from family and friends. Most 9s experience this because of the amount of travel they or loved ones undertake, and as your birthday is the pure form of 9, you may endure this more than other 9s.

Your pure 9 is the 'mirror' number in everything: with this birthday you have a capacity for clairvoyance, acting and counselling, since you can absorb and then reflect many people's experiences as if at first hand. This gift either amazes or disgruntles people.

You are artistic, possessing, in particular, literary, painting and musical skills. At work, you need an intellectual challenge. Any area connected with drama, writing, travelling, teaching, law, advertising or foreign affairs will be good, but if you stop and realise that your greatest chance of happiness will come from helping others out, there is no end to what you may achieve.

In the tarot, the number 9 card is the Hermit, and there is an aspect of this in your character, too; the man who has achieved wisdom through self-sacrifice and long years lived in the mind, offering service and illumination to the world. You also have a clear need for privacy at times.

BIRTHDAY ON 18TH

A birthday on the 18th indicates an intellectual mind, a traveller, an emotional and understanding character and someone who needs regular change. You can be very fond of an argument and will love your own independence. You have an ability to reach the public, are good at giving advice and have the tenacity to stick to a task until the job is completed.

You might well be quite conservative in thought and business, also good at handling or saving money. You must try not to be too critical of others, especially those who cannot learn things as quickly as you. Be positive and uplifting instead, and impart your good advice lovingly and humorously rather than offensively.

You are a lover of music, have a true appreciation for literature and may be well-educated and well-read. You have an in-born flair for the dramatic and would be a good writer of true-to-life fiction with this birthday, you will be subjected to constant and unexpected changes and the possibility of much travel in your life. If you do not travel in actuality, you will travel in your mind, or through books and other media. This may even take the form of day-dreaming – travelling away from a situation you are forced into and escaping in the mind.

Businesswise you could succeed at anything offering you scope, particularly politics (as you have the 'big brother' role in life), art, acting and law. You might well be fortunate dabbling in stocks or property, obviously a career in travel would make sense, and you will be a born counsellor and good listener in any job. Your base number, 9, is the clairvoyant number, so your intuitions and feelings will rarely be wrong.

BORN ON 27TH

Those born on the 27th are in the main delightful to be around, as the 2 in the birthdate puts other people first much of the time. This 9 has literary taste, wisdom, an innate spiritual understanding and a very strong psychic awareness. You may be poised and reflective, able to understand the feelings of others so deeply that you grieve for those in pain as though they were family. You are tranquil on the outside but also very determined and idealistic, and you can be nervous and erratic.

Once you have decided on a course of action you do not like to be challenged. You are a leader and will not enjoy working for others. You will work happily under your own steam or at the head of a group, where you will be a good motivator for others. You must be careful to avoid surrounding yourself with negative people, however, as this will affect you personally and you will take on their misery.

You have a very strongly developed musical, dramatic and literary ability. You may be fascinated by the mysticism of past cultures, drawn to the East and feel comfortable with metaphysical matters. You are deeply affectionate, but must guard against disappointment when others cannot return your intensity of emotion.

You will be a traveller and may even decide to live abroad. Like all 9s, you will have an interest in law, music, theatre, journalism, medicine, art and counselling.

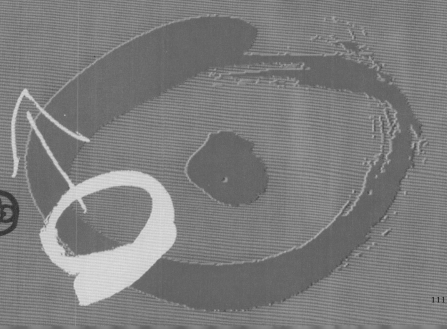

BIRTH FORCE 9

To find your Birth or Life Force number, add up all the digits of your birthday, including the month and year, and reduce them to a single number. The characteristics of this number will exercise its influence over your character gradually.

After many years of life and experience you will see the number 9 pattern assert itself in many ways. You begin to feel a strong sense of interest in humanity, a concern for world affairs and the cultures of other people. You want the best from your life – and a life lived completely, no matter how brave this demands you to be on occasions. Your soul and heart are deep; things affect you powerfully. Music touches a nerve right in your inner being, as does exceptional poetry or writing, or well-conceived drama and film. You can enter into an experience wholly and you love to feel these different emotions and moods as part of your growing awareness.

Number 9 rules the broadened mind, so you will make education, for yourself and for your children, a priority. Many mature students are 9s and even if your early education was broad you are quite likely to take up a specialist interest in a completely new subject as you get older.

You have a generous nature and a kind fellow-feeling towards friends and even acquaintances. You hate to see suffering and will do all you can to alleviate this in any way. You also have the gift of oratory, so you can sway others to understand your views and where help is needed. To some extent you seek perfection in yourself and others, but you are often aware that the achievement of this is not always possible; yet you will still carry on and get the best job done in the circumstances.

You develop a feeling of responsibility for people, which can be a heavy load to bear. You are so impressionable that you feel it personally when something is at odds around you: much time will be devoted selflessly to community needs or charitable works, not from guilt, but from a true wish to free people from unfairness and disabuse wherever possible. You are able to counsel and inspire other people, but be careful not to drain yourself.

One part of your personality becomes increasingly idealistic and even romantic; you hope for the best in everything. The other becomes progressively seasoned to disappointments and expects to be unsettled just at the moment of the most comfort and security. You gradually take on a spiritual dimension, largely because of the vicissitudes you have experienced, and become an example others will follow. The more tests you face, the more strength and spiritual beauty you discover in yourself.

You can understand concepts that most of us mortals find very difficult to wrestle with: as you live out the 9 number you appreciate more than anybody the cyclical nature of things. You learn to let people go with sadness and understanding. You are not a pessimist, for all this, but merely accept the need to shed a skin like a snake and grow a new one.

Your negative qualities include a tendency to be too restless and changeable, too moody, and even too quick to temper. Sometimes, though, your patience may just have been stretched too far. Perhaps after years of trying to tie yourself down you have come to understand that you need flexibility and freedom in both business and your personal life.

A love relationship that works for a 9 will be with someone who reads your moods and cheers you when you are tired. It will involve someone who likes to go away even for short weekend breaks and who is prepared to let you read a book, magazine or newspaper without feeling left out.

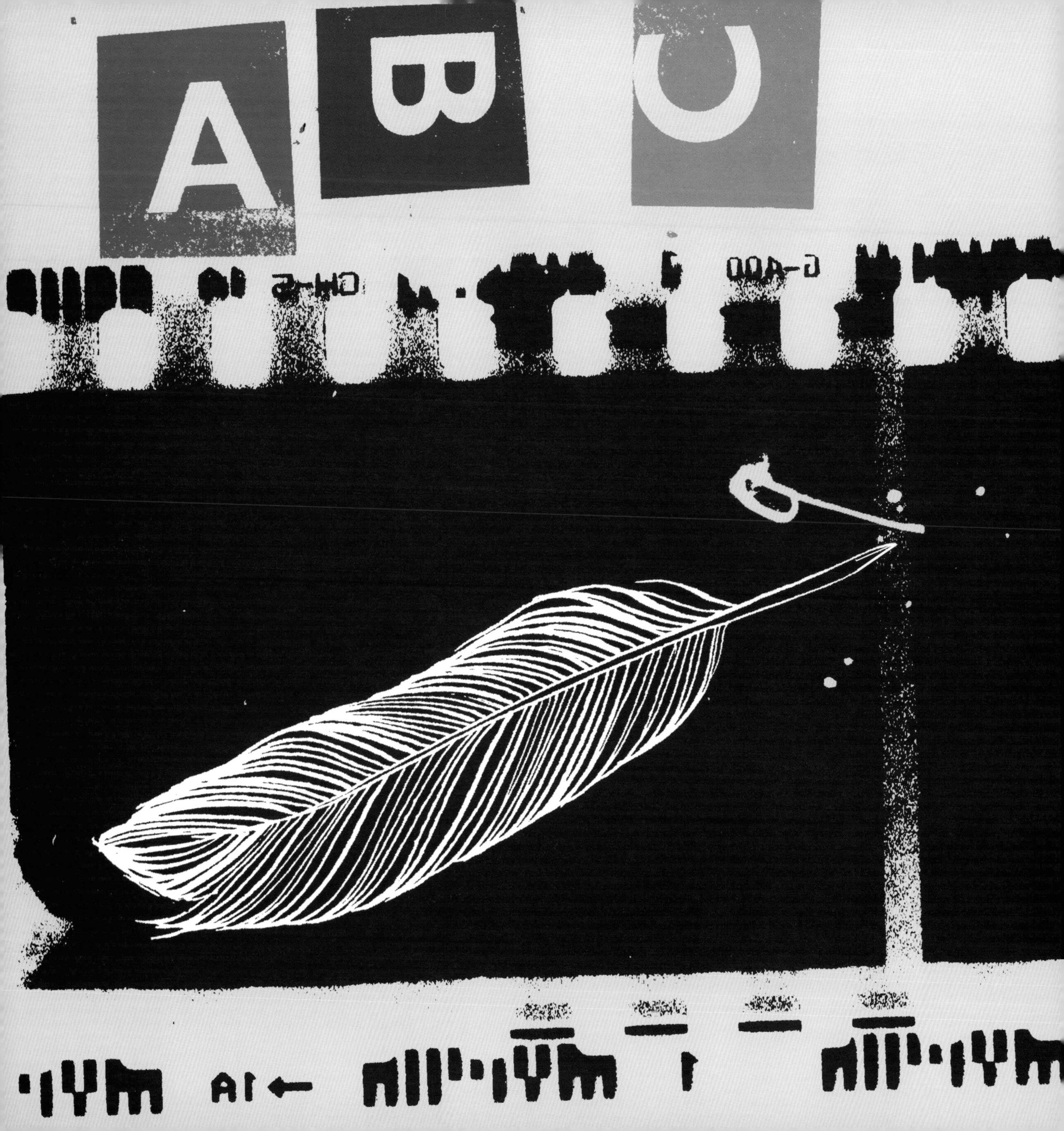
A
B
C

YOUR 9 LOVER

You have been drawn straight to this huggable, loveable soul. A 9 is always popular, having friends from every walk of life, it seems, and you are tantalised by this facet of his or her character. Everywhere you go – almost in any country – your 9 attracts people easily and bumps into long lost friends. Your 9's experience of life is far-reaching; he or she is generous and has wonderful and varied ideas about how and where to spend leisure time; you are proud of his or her well-informed, wise mind.

The best qualities in your 9 are a true selflessness and identification with other people's difficulties. All your friends want their advice, as they've seen or heard it all before and know how to rally a tearful girlfriend or cheer up a brother who's just been dumped. A hug from a 9 will soothe savaged nerves. But occasionally you must be prepared to put your foot down gently, if your lover unthinkingly neglects your needs while he or she falls victim to every sad story going.

Your 9 always forgives you when you react too vigorously to a situation, and is full of compassion when you want to whinge about a stressful day. And who can be moody when he or she is such a good storyteller and mimic? You may also be drawn to your 9's many capabilities: he or she can seemingly turn their hand to anything. They are painter, musician, writer, talker, actor; they are lucky with their cash and will share with everyone; they enlarge the canvas of your own opportunities by enticing you on to bigger events, foreign places, new situations that you may not have discovered yourself. You could never be bored with a 9.

Buy your good-looking 9 lover artistic clothes which accentuate his or her sense of drama and humour; he or she likes to dress in comfortable but interesting styles and may really like an ethnic look. Choose books, CDs, luggage or weekend breaks to appeal to the lover of surprise and variety.

But (and this is a big 'but'), sometimes your 9 seems determined that your relationship cannot last, because he or she has suffered so many previous heartbreaks. You may have to accept a rolling, moody nature in this situation – days when it seems that he or she expects the worst ultimately. If you are offering security, do so gently and you'll eventually succeed. You must be prepared to show that you aren't just a man or woman of straw.

THE 9 CHILD

A 9 baby is a gift: you can look forward to a beautiful and loving relationship with this wise little being. Your 9 is affectionate, compassionate, kind to others, romantic, thoughtful and bright. She or he is musical, naturally artistic, has good taste and enjoys reading and studying (lucky you). In fact a 9's mind must be expanded from the beginning, so he or she will benefit from trips to museums and galleries, houses and foreign countries. A 9 child picks up other languages easily, so encourage this multi-lingual streak.

Your 9 will ask intelligent questions about religion and politics, so don't fob them off with childlike replies, for they grasp the bigger picture and really want to know. Nurture your 9's relationship with his or her father, for this will be very important to them in later life, either being the strongest of relationships or lamented for its absence. If there are not great confidences between them there will be great misunderstandings.

Don't worry if your 9 is shy at first: the passing years will provide an education that will make it possible for them to draw on their great skills with people. It may just take a little time to grow into these abilities and understand the nature of their power. In time you will find your 9 completes the projects he or she starts.

THE 9 EMPLOYER

A broadminded individual for whom anything goes. You won't be judged for what new image you've adopted today, nor what sort of company you keep. A 9 boss expects you to be good to the whole team, be flexible in what you're asked to do and be ready to lend a hand when someone else is in crisis – it's no more than they would do themselves. Of course, a 9 may not always be there as travel comes so often with the number; but whether you have much free time or not, you'll probably end up liking this wise, kindly person.

THE 9 EMPLOYEE

Perfect: they're willing to do anything. In fact, they hate doing the same thing over and over, so give them lots of different jobs to do and their dexterity will amaze you. A 9 gets on with everyone in the office and is also happy to put in time socially when required. He or she is kind and sensible, having a pragmatic view about life overall. Provided they're stimulated, you will also find them to be hardworking.

THE 9 HOUSE

A place you will always travel from. The owners of 9 dwellings are rarely at home; the house itself has repeated changes of look and often inhabitants. Without wishing to be unsettling, you may find this is not the home in which you'll live out your days.

THE 9 LETTERS

Only the letters I and R are under the number 9. If you're a 9, you should have one of these letters in the name you use to bring out the best of your artistic ability and your capacity to ride out changes without getting distressed. If your first name begins with one of these letters, you are working with some of the qualities of number 9: excellent intuition, a love of the arts and the ability to finish what you start. If you are entirely lacking one of these letters, you may be intolerant of humanity, or lacking personal intuition.

THE 9 PET

Gets on with everyone and a great traveller. This lordly creature enjoys being taken on long walks, car journeys and even weekends or holidays away. A very wise little character.

WHAT HAPPENS IN A 9 YEAR?

Find the year cycle you are in by adding the numbers of your birth day and month to those of the current year (not your year of birth). This twelve-month cycle will run from one birthday to the next. The 9 year itself brings to completion a cycle of nine years, so change is inevitable.

This is a year of thought and clearing out. During this period you will see what is requisite to your future and be ready to let go of old baggage which is not part of your future life. Thus, a 9 year brings endings and separations, often with time needed to think through your final selections and space to dwell on what you want from the following years of your life. Many matters may come to a head, notably in business but also in relationships. A 9 year is therefore sometimes unsettling because change is the order of the day and you must be ready to roll with the punches. It is a test of your capacity to shake off encumbrances.

This is the time to finish positively any projects that are left over from previous years, but don't initiate new ventures until next year, when you will be directed by a new 1 year cycle. Until then, make an effort to tidy up the backlog and divest yourself of loads you may be carrying that are not in your favour. This could be a friendship that always drains you, a job that is no longer satisfying or a relationship which has run its course and has no real longevity. If you have been flogging the proverbial dead horse at any level, this is the moment to be honest and move forward unfettered. If you don't do it yourself, change will probably be forced upon you.

The sense of completion which takes place with this number is not necessarily connected with loss: it may well be just the opposite – a reward for working right through to the end of something. The appearance of a number 9 cycle could be exactly what you want, for with it you may see the welcome completion of years of hard work, which may be preparing you for your new life ahead. It could be the end of a long period of study, ushering in a new freedom now that your education is nearing the end; or it might be that you have been working on a house or a business for many years, finally bringing it to a proper state of readiness whereafter you can lead a new life without all this 'building work' going on.

Life sometimes throws a few obstacles at you under this cycle, because 9 demands wise and strong behaviour, but you have good intuition about what is happening. Just watch your health and be prepared to slow down. This is a good time to clear out the debris of your life; but do so gently, taking the full year to accomplish it. While this is happening, let new ideas clarify and tuck them under your pillow for next year.

Be open-minded during this year cycle: 9 is the broad thinker and this quality will be demanded of you in some way. Go with the flow: if you try to fight the rhythms that are working around you, trouble and pain may result. Flexibility is all. Changes and situations arise very swiftly; the mirror of the future may be trying to show you what is a hopeless project to be rid of, as well as what will be of use in the years to come.

Under the number 9 you must embrace your own future freedom or, if you are holding someone else back (it may even be a child who wants the experience of going abroad for the first time alone) you must be prepared to free them. Travel is a wonderful healer now, for it gives perspective; and the number 9 brings travel anyway. Travel helps you to distil those vital thoughts which preoccupy your mind on both an emotional and career level, so take up an invitation to go away, or be prepared to go on your own for a change of scene. A 9 year brings a more significant kind of travel than a 5 year, which often just indicates a quick trip.

Strong relationships need not fear the 9 cycle: these will strengthen and may even reach a stage of commitment, as this is fulfilment and completion of what has been growing. You may also find that old friends come back into your life during this number's reign. But if a relationship is living under a sentence of death, you will know that fully during this year. frightened and try to hang on to the past: letting go will free you for something fabulous next year.

ELEVEN

THIS IS OUR FIRST MASTER NUMBER: IT IS NEVER REDUCED
TO 2 BECAUSE THE POWERFUL PROPERTIES OF THE PAIR OF
LINKED 1S, THOUGH THEY HAVE AN UNDERCURRENT
PERSONALITY OF 2, ARE AT ODDS WITH THE GENTLE, PASSIVE
2. THEY HARNESS THE STRENGTHS OF TWO 1S, AND HAVE
THE SAME ENERGIES AND AGGRESSIONS WHILE THEY ALSO
HAVE THE SPIRIT OF 2. CONFUSED? THAT IS WHY THEY ARE
TREATED DIFFERENTLY...

    NUMBER 11'S BUSINESS IS TO LOOK TO THE PLANS OF THE
WORLD; IT IS ALWAYS REACHING BEYOND THE PERSONAL,
BEYOND THE MUNDANE, BEYOND THE EVERYDAY. IT IS A
TESTING NUMBER FOR ITS HOLDERS, WHO MUST LEARN HOW
TO HANDLE LIVING WITH TWO NUMBERS. IT DOES NOT
USUALLY BRING PERSONAL STABILITY, AND DEMANDS GREAT
MENTAL POWERS, STRENGTH OF CHARACTER, PHILOSOPHICAL
SELF-DISTANCING FROM LIFE SOMETIMES. HOWEVER, IT ALSO
BRINGS DEEP TALENTS, EXTRAORDINARY INSIGHTS AND HUGE
PERSONAL STAMINA. IT IS THE NUMBER OF INTUITION,
WISDOM AND EXCEPTIONAL PERFORMANCE.

    THE ONLY LETTER CORRESPONDING TO 11 IS K; ITS
COLOURS ARE FOREST GREEN, BLACK AND SILVER; IT HAS A
RAINBOW OF SCENT, REPRESENTING FULL SENSORY AWARENESS:
CHAMOMILE (FOR PEACE), LAVENDER (FOR HEALING), GRAPEFRUIT
(TO CHEER OTHERS), PEPPERMINT (SELF-ACCEPTANCE AND
CLARITY), HYACINTH (ENLIGHTENMENT AND PERSEVERANCE),
MARJORAM (COURAGE), JASMINE (SENSUALITY AND WELL-BEING),
PATCHOULI (COUNTERACTING MOOD SWINGS), ORRIS (FOR
COMMUNITY FEELING), SANDALWOOD (MEDITATION), AND
ROSEWOOD (OFFSETTING RESTLESSNESS). THE CORRESPONDING
ASTROLOGICAL SIGN IS AQUARIUS; AND AN 11 YEAR CYCLE
BRINGS MASTER ASSOCIATIONS AND POWERFUL INSPIRATION.

Day Force 11

This will be your number if your birthdate, leaving out the month and year in which you were born, is the 11th or 29th of any month. Either would give you the daily influence of this powerful Master Number, which will demand so much from you but also offer you the chance of having an exceptional life of high achievement and insight.

All 11 Birthdays

You do not understand the word 'impossibility'. For you the world is a storehouse from which you can draw any dream and make it your own, ask anyone (even in the highest office) for information, attain any post or place of dwelling without ever considering that it may be beyond reach. You work on deep levels of intuition, knowing at a glance whom to trust and what project is sound or a waste of time; and you have the most original mind of all numbers – drawing on the creative originality of number 1 with 2's power to get on with the job quietly.

You must be the leader in your group or business. As a child you would have been bored by plodders and wished for adult status immediately. You recognise no class or capability differences between yourself and anyone – which can sometimes border on rebelliousness. You are destined for mastery – but only if you use your gifts fully. An 11 can be like a high-IQ child, who is immensely bright but sometimes lazy. You need to be challenged, and you must push yourself hard. Then, the sky is the limit.

You are both sceptical of what sounds irrational and perceptive of what may appeal in a visionary kind of way. This trait can motivate others wonderfully, and you are a superb educator or public speaker, whipping up enthusiasm amongst otherwise inert or undirected people. Your fate should be to become famous, or at least widely known within bounds, but this fame should be for the public good, not for self-glory. Get this balance right and your life will be rich (in every sense) beyond measure.

You have an interest in law and, with your two numbers yoked together, see both sides of a dispute. You are zealous and may feel compelled to tackle injustice in a verbal way. After some years of going for a fight you will gain wisdom and know better how to achieve your ends. Honesty and fair dealing are imperatives for you.

Your number is highly emotional: you feel everything acutely. This makes you precocious in love when young, but inclined to overwhelm the object of your affection. You are a steam train, needing a strong and steady companion who can cope with your high electricity and unshakeable determination. Your lover must stand back and watch you, for getting in your way is a dangerous business. This can cause you emotional grief, as you can be self-destructive in relationships, being highly strung and demanding too much. Only time may show you how to deal with this.

You also go to extremes in business and intellectual interests; you will learn nothing by half. As such you could make a fortune many times, but you may lose it and have to start all over again. This is just one of the tests of your Master personality that life insists on throwing at you. Don't be tempted to use your charisma and high intelligence in a negative way, for it will come back to haunt you. Be as generous and high-minded as possible: this too will become your reward in return. The more you give (and you will be called on to give much) the more you will receive.

Follow your instinct to investigate the occult or alternative philosophies. You are tolerant, interested in varied views, and will find a path that helps you through tough times without becoming a crank about your beliefs. Others will often be jealous of you – for you are different, even exotic, and not everyone will be comfortable with this. Remember, the challenge of your number is to get those two digits in 11 into balance. Also, be prepared to do much for humanity without necessarily expecting anything in return – but selfless work is usually rewarded in the highest way.

BIRTHDAY ON 11TH

Born on the 11th, you have a pure Master Number birthday. This is both good news and bad, as carrying this number anywhere in your personal numbers brings added responsibilities and tests along with added possibilities.

You are born with great determination, but your wishes and wants may fluctuate. You would be at home in the limelight – indeed would come alive in this situation – and you must allow yourself plenty of scope to express your inspirational ideas. Try to focus your attention and concentration so that you may be an achiever rather than just a brilliant dreamer.

You are probably nervous, a perfectionist and very highly strung, though to the outside world you may appear calm and centred. You are truly psychic, visualising things clearly and having strong gut instincts about people and situations. Try to bring your intellect and intuition into balance. You will have a high moral standard, which could be conservative; guard against imposing these moral attitudes on others too stringently.

Your emotions are extreme, and you care deeply and protectively for your loved ones. You may astutely criticise others, but will take deep offence if anyone criticises those closest to you. You are certainly out of the ordinary, with an excellent imagination. You must be careful of self-deceit, however, and try hard to distinguish fact from fantasy. Of course, what is truth and what is illusion may form the nucleus of a very interesting debate for you.

You can succeed in literally any field which puts you before the public, ideal mediums being radio or television, music/dance/theatre, philosophy, art and art history, film, lecturing, advertising or PR. Equally, anything which gives you the opportunity of running your own business, preferably in something unusual and not too nine-to-five. Humdrum work will kill your spirit and make you lazy: it may even make you a cynic and a poor friend. You must strive for something special all the time in order to do the best by your great talents.

Remember, your number is the synthesis of the power and courage inherent in number 1, with the persuasive skill and sensitivity of number 2. The conjoined gifts should enable you to make a real mark on the world in your life, but will also confer double the responsibility.

Born on 29TH

The 29th is the other 11 Master Number birthday. You can achieve more in this lifetime, but you will also face daily tests along the way. Your true destiny would place you before the public. You are an idealist and a dreamer, but you have also a great capacity for leadership. You are probably spiritually inclined and have instinctive wisdom and philosophy.

This can be a very prosperous Day Force number if wisely used. The correct course for any Master Number is to help others; so you must walk a straight path and help friends to do the same. You will be inclined to moodiness, depression and nervousness and must cultivate the art of relaxation. This is especially true in matters of the heart for, like all the 'double digit' numbers, you will be extreme in your emotions, and will affect others with your moods. You must learn to live in the real world, with a mortal human for a partner rather than a god. Be wise about yourself, here.

You have a tendency to worry and over-analyse, and can be self-willed. You must also avoid a propensity to be so enthralled in your own world that you ignore others' strife. Try to remain calm and balanced. You will love all the beautiful things in life, and need a stable and sympathetic home to come back to. You will have many friends. You can convince anyone of anything if you've a mind to, but must fight intolerance of those who cannot grasp things as quickly or as easily as you. It is possible for you to have a hugely successful life, provided you remember the feelings of others.

You should have a public career, such as acting, politics, public relations, music, lecturing, selling and marketing. But you could also bring your own brand of professionalism to office management, writing or art. Again, like those with birthdays on the 11th, you must take care to utilise the dual powers of originality and individuality which come from the 1s in your number, with the ability for tact and consideration of others that comes from 2, your base number.

BIRTH FORCE 11

Your Birth Force, taken from the addition of all your birthday numbers – day, month and year – will show its influence over many years in your life, so you may not understand the true nature of the number in your personality until you have attained experience and wisdom.

With 11 as your Life Lesson number, you will be tested by difficult circumstances over the years, forcing you to dig deep and find out what you're made of. You expect the most of yourself and of others, like a 7, but you are irritated by the idea of doing things slowly and carefully, wishing for fast results like the number 1. So, in order to achieve those very high standards you seek, you must also learn patience. At the same time, you will frequently find that you are in a position which forces you to think quickly, eliciting an almost intuitive, rather than considered, response to events which are of the utmost importance.

You are a highly original and inspired human being, but you may not understand this for years. It begins in childhood, when you are expected to grasp very philosophical issues and, perhaps, cope with parental tension, much change, or a high degree of maturity which may be thrust on you if one parent is often absent. You do have a vast amount of courage, though, and if you are told by anyone that you cannot do/survive/cope with any situation, you will be stubborn in the extreme to disprove them. You learn leadership and personal strength through tests; you will discover astonishing talents in diverse directions. You have chosen a life which demands a degree of perfection, yet this is because it will bring out the best performance from you. And so it shall prove.

Throughout life, your intuitions will be of the most assistance to you, and you must learn to follow your nose in so many things. You want to push forward the frontiers of the known world (like the number 1), and you have the instinct to sniff your way on to the next phase of human development. If you are really functioning at the best your number has to offer, you will further the cause (whatever that may be) within your field of interest or business. The trick is to find the right balance between your material and physical urges on the one hand, and your spiritual and intellectual urges on the other: your emotions are caught up in both.

Across your lifetime your emotional stability will be tested again and again, for you are at odds between your rational nature, which sees all perfectly clearly, and your emotional needs, which may be quite fragile. The best way to endure this is to follow one clear ambition, which is of such importance to you that it will keep you focused even when those strong emotional winds blow. When you have discovered how to utilise your exceptional charm and glamour, intellect and originality, you will understand how to draw what you need in love. The world is out there for you, and it can become your playground if you are not distracted by emotional high waters.

For many 11s the ability to realize any dream they like, to achieve any ambition, is hollow without personal happiness or spiritual direction. The answer here comes with the passing years; as you understand how to govern your feelings and react calmly to those you love – rather than dramatically, as you may do in your early life – you will gain a balance in all things. Your emotional life can be fulfilling, you will control your money and you will explore your artistic gifts fruitfully. Putting the base urges aside will help you to live by pure inspiration.

Your talents careerwise should bring you before the public as actor, performer, speaker, lecturer, writer, or inventor. The difficulty in delineating the talents of an 11 is in knowing where to stop: in truth, you can turn your hand to anything which fascinates you. This can be a handicap, for you may cast your net too wide, or lose interest in something once you have established that you can do it. These flaws must be ironed out if you are to feel you have lived fully. Remember your capacity to inspire, and look upon this as a duty. If you discharge it, your life will truly be a happy one.

YOUR 11 LOVER

You fell in love at once with the star qualities of your 11. Here is an individual, pure and simple. No-one else is quite like him or her. An 11 has a style of their own, dressing originally in a look that is peculiar to them, defying rules, yet setting trends. Your 11 is refined and inspiring, diversely talented, a perfectionist, standing out from the crowd in all things. He or she has a wonderful humour, a vital mind, a huge degree of personal energy and powerful magnetism; and they do not do the jobs, or think the thoughts, or settle for the horizons, that other people do. They probably really deserve your attraction and love.

If you have found an 11 who has already grappled with some of the inevitable tests of personal strength and courage in their life, then you may have a very special human being here. He or she may already be famous, or heading towards fame; they may already know what they must do to lead an inspired life. They will be seeking, always; they will be innovative; they have grand ideas about what is possible and they intend to show they can achieve them. Your 11 lover is visionary and sparkling, a character apart, affectionate and emotional, determined to do something important in life.

In love, an 11 is full of fervour and individuality. His or her feelings are rarely tepid and in their wooing of you they can be inspired. Weekends in Venice, lunch in Paris, picnics on rooftops, Christmas shopping together in New York – no matter where you live, these are all perfectly logical expeditions for this person whose world knows no bounds. He or she is an inventive lover, one step ahead of you all the time. A natural love of luxury suggests champagne cooling next to the bed and a lovely blend of massage oils. Nor will they dress without thought – from outer to underwear. This should be a colourful and intense relationship.

Where you must be on your guard is for the sudden mood which appears before you have understood what provoked it. An 11 is so sensitive, and not nearly as self-confident as you thought. He or she is very idealistic and may have placed too much expectation on your capacity to return their feelings. If you let him or her down a touch, you may be unable to retrieve the situation, largely because of the idealised view of you that your 11 held. Be very patient, and hope that this exceptional human being has already grown into a mature understanding of love. It will come, but many heartbreaks line the path to that lasting love.

THE 11 CHILD

This number is testing for a child. It is so demanding, and bestows such a degree of dreaming, such a rich imagination, that your 11 may spend many years seeming to utter all sorts of unlikely scenarios for their future life. An 11 wants fame and wealth and power, but significantly, if they do learn to focus, they will achieve this.

The number places strain on the child because it is such an adult number: 11s must learn to govern their weaknesses – distraction, boredom, the temptation to daydream and build castles in the air – which they will only do as life toughens them. This often means that in childhood they are trying to grow into a huge and heavy, though impressive, mantle. They will stand out among their peers and either be incredibly popular or not understood at all. They may be eccentric and seem to their friends to be unrealistic. In hindsight this should not prove so, but it is a tall order for an 11 child to be seen as a grown-up and taken seriously.

Your 11 is extremely intelligent, but will be bored if tasks are too mundane. Therefore set out to challenge your progeny, give them a degree of difficulty and urge them to be resourceful. As they gain independence and control their heart and temper they will astonish everyone. Let them read widely, travel, and talk to adults; and, above all, try to help your 11 to feel emotionally secure. You have the responsibility: you are the parent of a Master Number. You must prepare him or her for the leading role they will play one day if they are to fulfil their potential.

THE 11 EMPLOYER

A true entertainer. You will marvel at your 11 boss, be inspired by him or her, learn from the seemingly effortless way they address others (especially at public meetings and conferences) and realise that they have some different, almost ethereal quality. The bad news is, they can be moody, suddenly lose heart for a demanding meeting because of unexpected stage fright, and expect a great deal from you too. However, this is mostly a generous and inspirational figure to work with, and the plus points way outclass the bad.

THE 11 EMPLOYEE

Another one waiting in the wings: while they are understudy, they are looking for a chance to showcase their own talents. This you may have realised, and are glad to harness their exceptional brain and drive for a quantified time. If, in fact, they look like being a future business partner, you are looking at great potential, for an 11 is the best, brightest, bounciest partner in the business.

THE 11 LETTERS

The only letter which corresponds to 11 is the 11th letter, K. It has all those properties of extremism, brilliance, imagination, charisma, that go with number 11. If your first name begins with K, or if your name boasts several Ks, you too will have the capacity to attract a richer fortune and more fame than usual. You are magnetic and original, creative, and probably have the focus to rise to the top. If you are an 11 but lack the letter K you may resent the demands and the intrusion placed on you by the world at large and will not be comfortable with your fame. Give yourself a nickname that includes a K in order to borrow the versatility and idealism of the letter.

THE 11 HOUSE

This place stands out in the street. It has some extra unusual characteristic which will attract a buyer or dweller who loves its eccentric features. It would make a marvellous investment but you may have to wait for it to endure swings in the marketplace. You may also find there are always jobs to be done in it to keep it in good shape. But you will feel special here; and, being also a kind of 2, it is a wonderful abode for a loving couple.

THE 11 PET

Even if you do not know your pet's birthday, you will know if you have an 11. This animal stands out among others, is charismatic, and is a star. Make sure you can live with this affectionate egotist.

WHAT HAPPENS IN AN 11 YEAR?

You should calculate each twelve-monthly cycle by adding the numbers of your birth day and month to those of whichever year you are currently in (not your year of birth). When this number adds up to 11, you are in for a demanding but highly rewarding year.

When you are in a Master Number 11 cycle you must be prepared for harder work with greater demands, but with the possibility of bigger rewards. This twelve-month spell is partly a learning period. You must be alert and watch for your opportunities. There are excellent prospects for success during this time, but much hard work is needed. You may be ignoring the powers and strengths you have, and should now look to ways of using your talent. Part of the problem could be that you worry about things that have no ultimate hold on your life: this could be costing you valuable time and energy. Don't waste time troubling over what you cannot change. Be prepared to move forward. If you can grasp this truth, the sky is now the limit.

You are full of insights and can evaluate opportunities in business and relationships shrewdly. Trust in yourself and listen to your inner voice; if you take advantage of your acumen you could rise quickly to the top and set yourself up for the future. There will be exciting business openings under this vibration and the chance perhaps to do something you have always wished to try. If you are an artist you may now get the chance to express your talents publicly. There might be educational opportunities and places in a course or school that didn't seem to be available before. Or, you may be in the right place at the right time to fill someone else's shoes in job terms, giving you the break you've always needed to show others what you can do.

The other important element of this cycle is finding a partner, either emotionally or in terms of work. You may meet someone who is completely different from anyone you have been involved with before, and you might need to be adaptable to cope with the implications of this. There is no room for fixed attitudes under this cycle. Flexibility is the name of the game, and although you will need to be somewhat determined to achieve your goals, yet you must be prepared to try hitherto unconventional paths to get there.

Perhaps, in regard to love, you have been in the habit of choosing the wrong people, partners who have no idea what you really want or how you think. You cannot confuse emotion with love under this cycle, for disappointments would soon come to light. Now you could find the perfect mate right under your nose, perhaps in the guise of someone you would never have considered before because you were too concerned with outward appearances. Look deeper and closer at everything at this time, and you may be surprised and delighted by what you uncover. The number 11 implicitly rules two people, so this could be a marriage vibration, or one bringing love and romantic joy if you are prepared to behave in a spirit of real harmony.

Some of the concerns of an 11 Master Cycle involve legal ties and contractual negotiations. It may be something straightforward, such as borrowing or purchasing a property; or perhaps you will inherit or be the recipient of a gift. Do be careful of contracts you sign: look through them carefully so you don't find yourself caught unawares later. Channel your mind, and work towards a co-operative arrangement with others.

If you allow yourself to be negative at this time, you will be plagued with fears and doubts, friends will let you down, and it will be almost impossible to arrive at decisions. Maybe the people who offer you help will have suspect motives, so look carefully at everyone, don't take anything for granted and don't accept anything at face value.

If you dig deep into your bag of talents you may surprise yourself by what you can do. You could discover what your abilities are worth by putting them to the test, and profit from your exploration. This is very much a time when peers or superiors recognise your talents and bestow honour and reward upon you. You have nothing to lose and everything to gain, so don't be lazy or shy. Go for it!

TWENTY TWO

OUR FINAL CHAPTER CONCERNS THE OTHER MASTER NUMBER, 22. LIKE NUMBER 11, IT ALWAYS VIBRATES TO THE DOUBLE DIGITS WHICH IN THIS CASE, BEING 2, GIVE IT THEIR CHARACTERISTIC FEMININITY AND CO-OPERATION WITH OTHERS, AS WELL AS BLESSING THE HOLDER WITH THE DEEP INTUITION AND AESTHETIC GIFTS OF NUMBER 2. AT THE SAME TIME, THE BASE NUMBER 4 – THE BUILDER, PRACTICAL, RATIONAL THINKER – OVERRIDES THE GENTLENESS OF THE 2S. THE EFFECT IS CONTRADICTORY – NOT QUITE SO MUCH AS FOR 11, BUT STILL ADMITTING A POWERFUL PERSONALITY WITH EXTRA INSIGHTS WHO IS BOTH A PUBLIC AND A PRIVATE PERSON: KNOWN, AND UNKNOWN, BY FRIENDS AND FAMILY.

22 IS THE NUMBER OF TRAVEL FOR EXPERIENCE, AS IT CORRESPONDS TO 'THE FOOL' (ALSO CALLED 'THE ADEPT') IN THE TAROT. PERHAPS FOR THIS REASON, MOST HOLDERS OF THIS NUMBER LEAVE HOME AND SEEK THEIR FORTUNE SOMEWHERE AWAY FROM THEIR PROTECTIVE FAMILY BASE: 22S OFTEN CHOOSE TO DWELL IN FOREIGN CITIES. THE NUMBER IS ALSO CALLED THE MASTER BUILDER: IT HAS THE BRILLIANCE AND PRECISION TO CARRY OUT THE MOST DIFFICULT AND AUDACIOUS OF PLANS, EITHER CEREBRAL OR PHYSICAL. MANY 22S ARE ARCHITECTS OR DESIGNERS ON A GRAND SCALE.

THE COLOURS OF 22 ARE WHITE AND GOLD; THE SCENTS ARE NEROLI (UPLIFTMENT AND STABILITY) AND PETITGRAIN (COMBATING MENTAL FATIGUE AND RIGIDITY). THE 22ND LETTER IS V; THE ZODIAC EQUIVALENT IS CAPRICORN.

AT THE END OF THIS CHAPTER YOU WILL FIND A SHORT NOTE ON NUMBERS 33 AND 44. THEY ARE ALSO MASTER NUMBERS, VARIANTS OF 6 AND 8, BUT ARE LESS FREQUENTLY RECOGNISED THAN 11 AND 22.

DAY FORCE 22

This is, as you know by now, the numbers of your birth day, not including the month and year in which you were born; in the case of 22, there is only one possible date on which you can be born, and that is the 22nd.

BIRTHDAY ON 22ND

The 22nd is a very powerful Master Number birthday. Your mind acquires facts and information as a matter of habit. You are both inspired and practical, imaginative and conservative. Like 11, the other double-digit birthday, you are nervous and highly strung, burning up a lot of frenetic energy; and you will need rest and seclusion from time to time. You must work on bringing your many talents into one cohesive whole; but with the continual operation of the two numbers you may sometimes lack focus.

22s usually leave their home town to achieve success, as they need the stimulus of unknown quantities. This should prove true whether your home town is quiet and slow, or cosmopolitan and internationally renowned: a Londoner might be as likely to turn up in New York, as someone from Arkansas to turn up in Washington. (Byron, born on 22nd January, lived all over the place.) You are very capable, having great personal power and magnetism: you must try to develop a tolerance for those who do not digest things as quickly as you. With your determination you can honestly accomplish anything you desire. You are the Master Builder and the Master Writer, but you must decide where you will direct your energies.

There is a strong humanitarian facet to your character, and you should use this to become global rather than parochial in your thinking. A huge number of famous people have this birthday and the best of them have done something worthwhile for the world. Use your intuition often, rely on your first impressions, for they will usually be right. As this is a double-digit number, everything will come to you in double measure – whether it be good or bad. If you live positively you will attract the best karmic responses.

You are witty and chatty when necessary, but this belies your depth and seriousness. For this reason you are often misunderstood, as much by yourself as by others. Develop your tact, expand your executive ability and work to organise others, particularly for the public good. Avoid your inclinations to laziness and extravagance.

You have the power to attract great wealth and powerful business influence across the globe: yours is more likely to be a business or creative life with international links than a concern in your back garden. No problem is too difficult to solve: you are able to do this because of the synthesising power of rational thought and cool, detached objectivity of your base number 4 harnessed to the power of diplomacy and gift for co-operative work with other people given you by the pair of 2s. You may even try to find ways of building a better world, on a small or large scale.

Your opinions are fairly fixed but have probably been arrived at by a large amount of suffering, analysing and acquiring wisdom. This may lead you into a career in politics, or at least an interest in the subject. Be aware, however, of the possibility of overwork inherent in your number: both 2s and 4s are hard workers, and 22 more so than both.

Your best fields of endeavour will be in writing or the use of words, foreign affairs, building, property, architecture, export, handling people, film directing, or other possibly unsung roles in show business and theatre. Fame is not the issue for you; rather, you want to see an impressive job done – one which will make a difference to the world you inhabit. Always, then, go for the project on the grandest of scales.

BIRTH FORCE 22

This will be the number guiding your direction in life, and is deduced from the total of all your birthday numbers: day, month and birth year. There will be many more 22 Birth Forces now that the Millennium has reduced the year numbers to the lower digit: 2+0+0+ whatever the final digit will be. Birthdays late in the 1970s, 1980s or 1990s are unlikely to create a 22, unless you were born in the first day or two of January or February.

With a Birth Force number 22, your keyword might well be vision. This may be a testing incarnation, where you must learn that service to others is the most rewarding form of work. You are inspired and spiritual instinctively, yet you love the good life. Your demand for high standards from yourself and others is ongoing. Try to learn new talents and be practical in what you wish to achieve.

Number 22 is the Master Builder. You have the imagination of an 11, but it is coupled with the enviable steadiness of a 4, so you may truly build from inspired plans. Part of your life's work will be to make money for the good of others. You could be a brilliant fundraiser, charity organiser or campaigner. You have the skills of a business executive. Try not to regard materialism as necessarily a bad thing. Business achievement can have a very humanitarian application.

You must learn to control your inclination to intolerance, especially as you see things quickly and easily but others may take longer to understand how things work. Try to co-operate with, and encourage, those who understand things differently from you. You could be a brilliant politician and a sensitive diplomat as you have the peacemaking powers of the number 2 working always within your number. Use your abilities on a grand scale.

The career possibilities for a 22 are too numerous to mention; basically, you can do anything you set your mind to. The best applications of your efforts may be toward the public good, and ultimately you will probably be in the public eye in some form or other.

Remember that your principal objective is to build something – be this in a material way or just metaphorically. Your life will be incomplete if you do not feel you have accomplished something. You should be ready to talk to those in power or with political authority; or you should be in a position of influence yourself. As you come to know yourself over the years, you will better understand how to employ your considerable gifts to get things done. You will ultimately find that you can handle your money and accounts well, and organise your life efficiently, though to start with you may have many tests to undergo which force you to learn to do this.

Don't feel guilty about wanting material security; it is requisite to your plans of setting out in the world to achieve. You will need to deal from a position of strength. Your goals are more ambitious than those of many people, and you deserve to be stable yourself in order to offer others more stability.

YOUR 22 LOVER

If you've fallen for a 22, you are looking for someone special. This is a lover who exudes power, originality and a rational but exciting mind. You perceive his or her innate powers of diplomacy and the masterly manner in which they glide through the world. They are on equal terms with absolutely everybody: no-one causes them fear or nervousness. Also, the world is quite literally their oyster: there are no boundaries in the world across which a 22 cannot jump.

Your 22 is probably already materially secure, or on their way to such security; the idea of choosing a high-earning career path and investing early in property is bread-and-butter to a 22. He or she will give freely to anyone deserving, be it a career break, advice to the broken-hearted, or money for an important cause. To do this, he or she has had to become stable and unshakeable first.

Carefully dressed in stylish clothes with a particularly original 'look', he or she will meet you for a date with a difference. You will not go somewhere over-popular, but subtle and stylish. You will often find travel on the agenda in a long-term relationship with a 22. Only a full experience of what the world has to offer will satisfy him or her, and you will be taken along for an amazing ride.

As a lover, your 22 is possibly less adventurous than other numbers; but you will be solidly cared for, and you're quite likely to be adored in beautiful surroundings in a nice home. Foreign cities will bring out the tiger in your lover, and because he or she is a double-digit number, you will find they have mood swings: one day they're really excited by love, on other days, far less so. Learn to read the mood.

To be with any Master Number can be difficult, as you share the physical person with the mental demands placed upon them by the world at large. They must fulfil something in themselves – a destiny that is pressured, ambitious, demanding – so you will need to be unselfish sometimes. The rewards are worth it: a stable relationship with an impressive personality who has their mind on weighty issues.

THE 22 CHILD

This is a difficult nurturing job in many ways. Your 22 is quite brilliant, wants to be grown up now, and yet must learn how to use his or her majestic powers of dealing with people, applying intelligence to puzzle solving, and even understanding what is going to be the most important thing, careerwise, in their future. All Master Number children want to be grown up too quickly, and all Master Numbers need experience in order to grow into a full awareness of their exceptional skills and needs.

You have here a small person capable of great observation and intuition, although he or she is also quite sceptical, too. It will take a lot to convince them, and a 22 child wants to live through a range of situations to draw anything of philosophical merit from them. So, your child will get into tight corners almost deliberately, just to see how to get out of them. He or she will espouse serious issues early on. You ought to give your 22 a good encyclopaedia to enable them to investigate the past; also let them browse the world on the web. This is a far-ranging mind.

The most frustrating aspect of your young Master Number 22 is their impatience with slower-minded humans. Try to teach them to realize that not everyone sees things their way, or with as much insight and speed. You have a powerful team of horses pulling on the reins in your 22: your job is to direct them, but allow them to unleash their power.

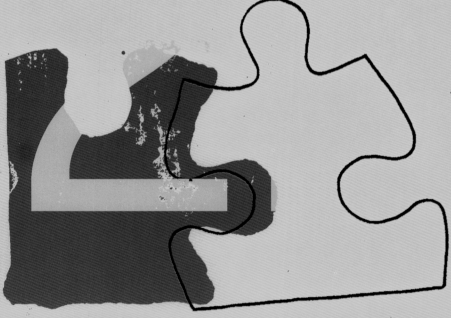

THE 22 EMPLOYER

A very stable person, who has hopefully ironed out their mood swings. This is a clever person who is basically old-fashioned but open to improved ways of getting things done. Ask for a new phone system or PC and you will probably be given it – if it looks as though it will ultimately lighten the load. Your 22 boss is sure to travel a good deal; in fact, were they born abroad?

THE 22 EMPLOYEE

This is a good person to have on board: hardworking, polite and self-assured. A 22 is going somewhere, likes to work in partnership and will learn something helpful every day of the week. They are the perfect team member, and delighted to deputise for you on trips away or at public functions when an address is required. Very reliable and bright.

THE 22 HOUSE

Undoubtedly designed by a master builder, this is a wonderfully sound structure, conservative in some respects, but certain to endure a veritable earthquake. It needs a garden as all 4s like the earth; and you may find you are often living abroad from it. However, the 22 house may last you through a whole lifetime.

THE 22 LETTER

The only letter vibrating to 22 is V, the 22nd of the alphabet. If your first name begins with this letter, or you have several Vs in your name, you have many of the characteristics of the masterminded 22. This letter goes with fixed ideas and strong opinions; oddly, its bearers are either very practical, or completely impractical. If you're a 22 you need a V in the name you use to help you express your excellence verbally, and to persuade people easily. Without a V, you may have too many emotional ups and downs and find your plans are never quite finalised.

THE 22 PET

A very solid animal who will quickly find out how life works and how to get the most from it. You'll find your 22 cat enjoying the best corner of your garden, or a 22 dog always roving around for the sake of knowing the whole community. These are the best animals to have in any kind of service to the community, such as guide dogs, horses for small children to learn to ride, and so on. Somehow, the epitome of a 22 animal would be a dolphin.

WHAT HAPPENS IN A 22 YEAR?

You will probably only enjoy a 22 year cycle once in your life, when all your relevant numbers – your birthday, month and the year you are currently in – add up precisely to 22. Most future cycles will be 4s. When this is the year number you experience, it is a moment when your dreams may all suddenly come true.

Depending on the way you handle yourself during your 22 cycle, expect this period to embody either folly or the utmost wisdom. Like the Major Arcana XXII in the tarot to which it relates, there is a dual interpretation for this number, and two possible courses it may run.

On the most mundane level, this cycle is still linked with mastership (22 is the second Master Number), so you are unlikely to think in anything but sweeping terms. If a job change is heralded, you will not simply swap one position for a similar one under this vibration: you will have ideas that affect many people and probably be offered the chance to show your worth in a top-ranking post. You will become the expert in your field. Your thinking is expansive and you won't stop until you know everything there is to know about what interests you. Superiors will acknowledge this and you will be given responsibility. Other people will seek your opinion and want your advice; you are confident enough to give it.

Travel is almost a certainty under this number. Chances are you will want to go somewhere which seems important, perhaps visiting an ancient civilisation rather than an island resort, or linking up with people who are important to you, wherever they may be. A journey undertaken now is likely to be one seeking something new, going to a destination which gives you a chance to see something entirely different, a trek which helps you discover new facets of yourself along the way. The money will somehow be there for you to undertake these adventures: your family might chip in, a raise or bonus might make it possible or luck will come from an unexpected source. If it is important that you go, a way will be found.

There are difficulties with this cycle, too. You may have such grand visions that folly is possible. Material matters may take on too much significance. Your wild and wonderful dreams may also be imprudent. You will experience excitement and tension, and you must guard against extremes. This is not the best time to speculate in any area of which you cannot be certain. Eschew gambling and be thoroughly practical.

One of the important aspects of this cycle is to be aware of your own limitations and consult professionals in regard to any matters requiring astute judgement. Once you have been presented with the facts, use your intuition to make final decisions. This is a powerful cycle, for good rather than ill, so long as you exercise good insight.

In some respects, when you look back later on this period you will see that you have made some extraordinary observation, some move, that changed everything in your life and moved you onto an altogether higher plane. You have extraordinary courage now, the ability to rush in where angels fear to tread – and you will land safely, as long as the basic motivation you had was without selfishness.

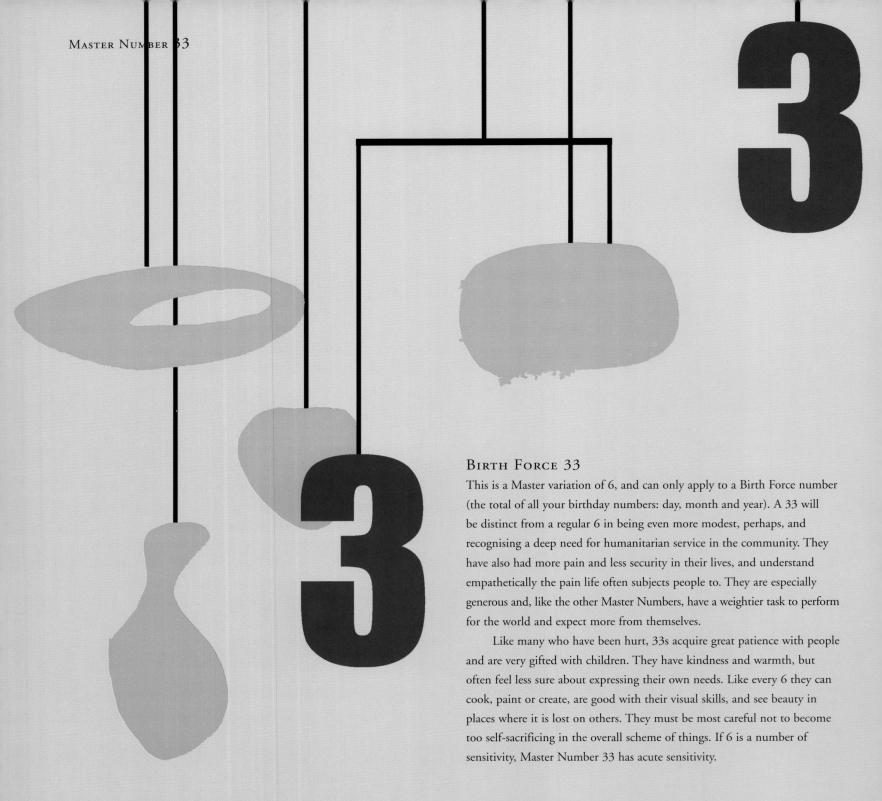

BIRTH FORCE 33

This is a Master variation of 6, and can only apply to a Birth Force number (the total of all your birthday numbers: day, month and year). A 33 will be distinct from a regular 6 in being even more modest, perhaps, and recognising a deep need for humanitarian service in the community. They have also had more pain and less security in their lives, and understand empathetically the pain life often subjects people to. They are especially generous and, like the other Master Numbers, have a weightier task to perform for the world and expect more from themselves.

Like many who have been hurt, 33s acquire great patience with people and are very gifted with children. They have kindness and warmth, but often feel less sure about expressing their own needs. Like every 6 they can cook, paint or create, are good with their visual skills, and see beauty in places where it is lost on others. They must be most careful not to become too self-sacrificing in the overall scheme of things. If 6 is a number of sensitivity, Master Number 33 has acute sensitivity.

Birth Force 44

This is the Master version of 8 and thus a very powerful achiever in the world. Again it is only a Birth Force, and its bearers will learn to handle the more demanding, higher number over the years. 44s gain extraordinary control in their lives and come to an astonishing and enviable balance between the spiritual and the material. An 8 must set the office and the house in order; 44 should set the world in order. This number is dedicated to the best that can be gained from material success, the most unselfish application of funds, and to any kind of business which has a spiritual and humanist dimension.

A 44 will instinctively seek a way of instituting better ethics in business and education, generating a powerful moral sense between people who share a roof of any kind. Brave and strong like their base number, 8, they are also musical, well-read and fair-minded. But, as a Master Number, they have experienced pain and much change in their lives. This gives them a sense of detachment, an understanding of what it is important to fight for and what is mere vanity. So, if you are a 44, you will only feel fulfilled by contributing something worthwhile to the world around you. You may experience degrees of difficulty in love, business and education, but this will simply engage your huge, deep capacity for survival and strength. Yours is a life which promises very great rewards but from considerable effort.

ONE	TWO	THREE	FOUR	FIVE	SIX
♥♥♥♥ Both wanting to take control, this could be stormy! But you respect each other's privacy and have similar mood swings. It is a number in common.	♥♥♥♥ A leader and a follower. 2 is sensitive to 1's ego and helps follow 1's ideas through well. Good potential.	♥♥ Two extroverts, but 1 wants more privacy than 3, and is irritated by 3's popularity with everyone. Jealousy could be a problem.	♥♥♥ Quite good: 4 is able to pick up 1's mess and organise him/her a little. But, 4s may seem too rigid and old-fashioned some of the time for a flamboyant 1.	♥♥♥♥♥ 5 is naturally drawn to 1's clever ideas and possibly improves on them. A very physical bond, but should work well – in the fast lane of life.	♥♥♥ Some tensions: 1 looks for stimulus, 6 for peace. Many friends come to be entertaine[d] by you both – but a good few miscommunications ahead.
	♥♥♥ As long as one of you takes charge sometimes, this is a peaceable union. Danger is that it may become humdrum and unadventurous. Perhaps that suits?	♥♥♥ More lively, but 2 needs stability that 3 can't really offer. This is potentially good for a sexy fling, with each drawn to the opposite qualities.	♥♥♥♥♥ Excellent! You understand each other's foibles and vulnerabilities, live in a neat space, and are both quite giving. You fire each other's creativity	♥ No! 2 is initially drawn to 5's dynamism, but grows weary of its child-like behaviour and inability to settle. 5 wants 2 to be more enthusiastic about life.	♥♥♥♥ Good scope: both of you arti[stic] love people, enjoy music and [...] You may need a push to get [...] off the ground, but could live (and work) well together.
		♥♥♥♥♥ Actually, a really good bond. You know how to pick each other up when one is down. Moody, but full of light and humour. Your home will be beautiful.	♥ More staid. 3 wants fun and variety, 4 stability and not too many changes. Not ideal. A constant friction between revolution and conservatism.	♥♥♥♥ Good for business: you charm everyone, and are lucky with money. In love, a good chance if you're both rich enough to enjoy your leisure time fully.	♥♥♥♥ A strong tie. You have many friends, love doing things, bu[t] also enjoy each other's dream [...] 3 needs mothering, 6 will do [...]
			♥♥ Solid, but possibly boring. No-one to get you out of the house or the office. You do understand each other well, and have a number in common, but no dynamics.	♥ Horses pulling in different directions. Good for friendship, as you see things so differently and can explain opposite views. In love, a lot of heartache.	♥♥♥ Better: 6 will help 4 relax a li[ttle] and make a good home for him/her. 4 can provide the stability and security 6 craves [...] It may descend to dullness.
				♥♥♥ Whew! Exhausting! A pair of clowns, who travel all the time (not necessarily together). Much in common, but the danger is, never together.	♥♥♥ Unsure. Better if the 5 is mal[e] the 6 female. One number fu[l...] dynamism and energy, the ot[her] artistic gentleness and a wish [...] peace. Challenging.
					♥♥♥♥ 6 and 6: Works very well. He[re ...] two numbers that really enjoy [...] other. You add complimentar[y] skills visually, and your home [is ...] joy to visit.

COMPATIBILITY

When consulting this chart, calculate your compatibility from a comparison of Day Forces (yours and the other person's) to see how you fare on a day-to-day basis, and then from your Birth Forces (again, yours and the other party's) to find out how you will get on over the course of many years. Don't mix and match, comparing your own Day number with your partner's Birth Force. However, let it be said that if you have either number in common with your partner, you have a powerful bond. This is true if, say, you each have a Day Force 3, or, if one of you has a Day Force 3 and the other a Birth Force 3. It is only relevant to cross match the numbers in this one instance.

The Heart Rating, out of 5, is a guide. 5 hearts suggests, obviously, great potential to work well together; but if you have only 1 heart, you will have to work harder to avoid damaging quarrels and misunderstandings.

	EIGHT	NINE	ELEVEN	TWENTY TWO	
...of a feather: both like privacy, ...ntellectual types, happy to do ...on your own and with each ...Good for business, too.	♥♥♥ This makes a strong friendship, but 8 loses patience with 1's inability to finish what it starts. A sporty, or physical bond, might help somewhat.	♥♥♥ Some common ground: 9 completes what ambitious 1 starts. A pioneer and a traveller, could be good together, and 9's boredom threshold may be held at bay.	♥♥ High water! Both volatile numbers who like their own way, an 11 may steal 1's thunder. More likely to be a short intense affair.	♥♥♥ Could work, as you both like taking chances and trying all possibilities. However, the Master Number loses patience with 1's lack of concentration.	ONE
...ng friendship, but not ideal ...g-lasting love. 2 gets on with ...ny people, 7 prefers some ...de, and is cross with 2 for ...ering everyone.	♥♥♥♥ Not bad at all. Both able to see two sides to an argument, this has potential of great fairness and humour as well. Lots of people come to you for advice.	♥♥♥♥ Again, quite good. 2 will back up 9's dreams and work towards the same goals, getting on with everyone. 2 may need to organise 9 sometimes.	♥♥♥♥ The Master Number will dominate, but the 2 may be happy with this. You are effectively two numbers in common, and the 11 will keep 2 laughing and busy.	♥♥♥♥♥ As good as 2 and 4. This is a love relationship, provided 2 is happy to take the back seat and navigate. You could achieve a very sound and loving tie.	TWO
...rriage of opposites, but can ...3 makes 7 laugh, 7 gets 3 to ...ntrate sometimes. One is ..., the other serious, but you ...reate a blend.	♥♥♥♥ A powerful relationship. 8 understands 3's gifts, and is generous about them, while 3 rallies 8's mood when there is too much pressure on. Good understanding.	♥♥♥♥ A bringing together of similar temperaments and humours. You will keep active, enjoy diverse friends and hobbies, and probably get on very well.	♥♥ Great sex: you love each other's kinkiness. On a day-to-day basis, not enough stability, too much conflicting ego. Likely to be high and then low.	♥ Not really. Both of you are headed for different lives. Enjoy the momentary variety, but be ready to call it a day eventually.	THREE
! These numbers have a ...deal in common: 7 will ...but 4 will help 7 through ...of confidence and ...onal pressure.	♥♥♥ Great for a business relationship, and not impossible for love. 4 needs to respect 8's charisma and determination, 8 to rely on 4's anchoring love.	♥ Problems! 9 can't keep still, 4 likes to tend its garden. 9 is spendthrift, 4 a born accountant. 4 is old-fashioned, 9 progressive. It could be a challenge!	♥♥♥ Yes! 11 loves to jolly up 4 and depends on 4's sound advice and unswerving love. 4 admires 11's courage and cleverness.	♥♥♥ Obviously one must lead, and it will be the 22. These are two numbers in common, good for relationships, powerful in business together.	FOUR
...rivate, 5 a people person. ...are intelligent, but in ...ent ways. Many good ...ssions ahead, but clashes and ...nderstandings too, I fear.	♥♥♥ Works rather better than you might think: both can be physical (5 always is) and enjoy new frontiers. 8 works very hard, 5 might wish for more holidays?	♥♥♥ Travel is common ground, but not a lot of stability here. You're a pair of clowns from different theatres. Not for love, but for brilliant friendship and sex.	♥♥♥ Possible. You have great charm (together) and wit, but may compete with each other for the limelight. Variety will be the crucial element.	♥ An entertainer and an impresario? Maybe. But one wants to be thoroughly organised, the other never tied down. 22 can't cope with 5's irrepressible youthfulness.	FIVE
...h. 6 is much more easy-going ...nds 7 critical, even brittle. 7 is ...by 6's lack of discernment and, ...ps, self-discipline. A storm ...g to break!	♥♥♥♥ Good potential. Both love music, creativity, people, money to spend. 6 creates a haven of good taste, 8 is happy to pay for it. Also, pretty good physically.	♥♥♥ This works. A powerful friendship which may develop into love. You have many things in common: similar taste, arts, theatre, friends.	♥♥♥♥ 6 keeps 11's dreams alive but also moulds them into realistic possibilities. This would be a good tie for a mature couple: very loving and wise.	♥♥♥ Not bad: 22 will appreciate 6's help and advice, and provide some stability for 6's domestic comfort. Some intrinsic differences of opinion inevitable, though.	SIX
...ear, a bit serious. Yes, these ...umbers in common, but 7 ...s some light relief and won't ...from another 7. A very ...y tie this.	♥♥♥♥ 7 and 8: Surprisingly good. Both superior intellects, both specialists albeit in different areas. This can work if respect is achieved; it is also very sexy.	♥♥♥ Much intellect in common again, though 7 would rather concentrate on certain friends and goals, 9 is more broadly inclined. Competitiveness may be a problem.	♥ A relationship of extremes, of high days and low days. 11 needs subtle coaxing and ego-boosting, while 7 is irritated by this. 11 wants so much, 7 prefers perfection.	♥♥♥ This may work if the 7 is allowed to take the lead sometimes. 22 has a sense of 7's fine mind, 7 realises 22 is no fool. Two individuals who may work well together.	SEVEN
	♥♥♥♥ Perhaps! These two numbers in common could be fantastic if their combined outlets were also harnessed for business. Volatile, though.	♥♥♥ A powerful friendship, though each sees the world differently. In love, the 8 will want the 9 at home more often than he/she is perhaps willing.	♥♥♥♥ You think similarly, both seeing the two sides of complex problems. You are also arty, adventurous, clever. Your common hobbies will make or break this.	♥♥♥ Excellent for business, but a little crunchy for love. You both like to have your way, and both have a point all the time, but not always the same point!	EIGHT
		♥♥♥ Prone to moods together. You will love travelling, reading, educating each other, but if one of you is feeling glum, the other follows. Could be bumpy.	♥♥♥ Better, but still volatile. This depends on who is in control, and whether the 9 sees the 11 as brilliant and charismatic. Maybe both of you are, but one must lead.	♥♥ Two sophisticates who will perhaps try to outdo each other. You're naturally drawn together, but will also annoy each other.	NINE
			♥♥♥ Oh – this will create magic or murder! You are certainly aware of each other's needs, but if you turn on each other, ouch! Give each other space sometimes.	♥♥♥♥ Much better than 11/11. Both Master numbers, you recognise each other's greatness, but also have enough differences to complement each other. Potentially very loving.	ELEVEN
				♥♥♥ This is business. Love has no place here: you're busy making a new world. Its hard to imagine time for romance, but you'll fascinate each other, certainly.	TWENTY TWO

To order a Personal Numerology Chart from Titania

If you would like your own Personal Numerology Chart drawn up by Titania we will be happy
to send you details of price and an order form. Please send your name and address to:

Titania Hardie Chart Order
c/o Quadrille Publishing Limited, Alhambra House
27-31 Charing Cross Road, London WC2H 0LS

Each chart will be individually co-ordinated by Titania and will consist of approximately
20 pages of information based on your birth date and full name. It will be divided into
three sections: a character analysis, future trends and your compatibility with other numbers.

Thanks as ever to everyone at johnson banks, especially Chris, and to Shonagh.
Thanks, too, to Anne, and to Rory, Gabriel and Samantha for adding ideas;
and hugs to all the Quadrille Jo's for everything sweet and smiley, especially
my lovely Jo Harris (wherever she may be). But most thanks go to the girls
this book is dedicated to.